This is Islam

New Revised Edition

Michael Keene

Stanley Thornes (Publishers) Ltd

Text © Michael Keene 1996, 1999

Original illustrations © Stanley Thornes (Publishers) Ltd 1996, 1999

First published in 1996.
This edition published in 1999 by:
Stanley Thornes (Publishers) Ltd
Ellenborough House
Wellington Street
CHELTENHAM GL50 1YW
England

99 00 01 02 03 / 10 9 8 7 6 5 4 3 2 1

A catalogue record for this book is available from the British Library.

First edition ISBN 0-7487-2558-X
This edition ISBN 0-7487-3903-3

Printed and bound in China by Dah Hua Printing Press Co. Ltd.

Acknowledgements

With thanks to the following for permission to reproduce photographs and illustrations:

Agence Photographique Hoa-Qui 19 ● Andes Press Agency/Carlos Reyes-Manzo 39 (bottom), 73 ● Bridgeman Art Library, London, New York/Bibliothèque Nationale, Paris: Fr 22495 f.235v Combat between the Crusaders and the Saracens in c. 1185, 14th century from Li Romans de Godefroy de Buillon et de Salehadin, 46, /Hermitage, St. Petersburg: Part of a large Infantry banner depicting the Last Judgement, Russian, 1695 (silk painted decoration), 50 ● Circa Photo Library/John Smith 42 ● Carl Gray 80 ● Sonia Halliday Photographs 7 ● Robert Harding/Susan Griggs Agency 56 ● Hutchison 37 (right), 38, 39 (top), 47, 68, 71, /Liba Taylor 30 ● The Islamic Foundation 44, 78 ● Christine Osborne 89 ● Rex Features Ltd 5, 37 (left), 69, 76, 86 ● Peter Sanders 9, 10, 11, 12, 24, 25, 32, 45, 52, 57, 72, 74, 77, 84, 85, 87, 92, 95 ● The Walking Camera 26, 28, 29, 31, 34, 35, 36, 40–41, 43, 53, 54, 55, 58, 59, 60, 61, 62, 63, 64, 65, 66, 67, 70, 75, 81, 82, 88, 90, 93 ● Jerry Wooldridge 33.

Every effort has been made to contact copyright holders and we apologise if any have been inadvertently overlooked.

Design and page layout by Janet McCallum.

Illustrated by Barking Dog Art, Hardlines and Gillian Hunt.

Cover artwork by Ian Kennedy.

Picture research by Julia Hanson.

Throughout this book the terms BCE (Before Common Era) and CE (Common Era) are used instead of the more familiar BC and AD. However, in practice, they mean the same thing.

Contents

What is Islam?

Islam is one of the most important religions in the world. The followers of this religion are called **Muslims**. They are part of the fastest-growing religion in the modern world. One out of every four people alive today is a Muslim. Only Christianity now has more followers.

Origins

Islam is a sister faith to Christianity and Judaism, since all three claim to have a spiritual link to the Prophet Ibrahim (Abraham). Muslims regard themselves, Christians and Jews as 'People of the Book'. This means that they believe that the revelations of God reached them through the prophets, including Ibrahim, Nuh (Noah), Musa (Moses), Isa (Jesus) and Muhammad. Muslims believe that there have also been other prophets – messengers of God who have brought God's guidance – and that Muhammad was the last of the prophets: there will be no other prophet after him.

Muhammad

Islam is founded on the revelations given to the Prophet Muhammad. These revelations are known as the Qur'an. There were earlier revelations which came to the prophets before Muhammad. The Qur'an says that it confirms and completes these revelations. Muhammad was born in 570 CE in the city of Makkah in Arabia. From Arabia, the influence of Islam flowed rapidly and strongly.

Today, Islam is a worldwide religion representing about 25 per cent of the world's population. Countries in the Middle East and North Africa, like Saudi Arabia, Iraq, Egypt, Tunisia and Libya, are mainly Muslim. So are many countries in Central Asia. Muslims also form a majority of the population in Indonesia, Pakistan and Bangladesh. There are almost two million Muslims in Great Britain alone.

Wherever Muslims are found they are united in their faith. All believe that there is no God but

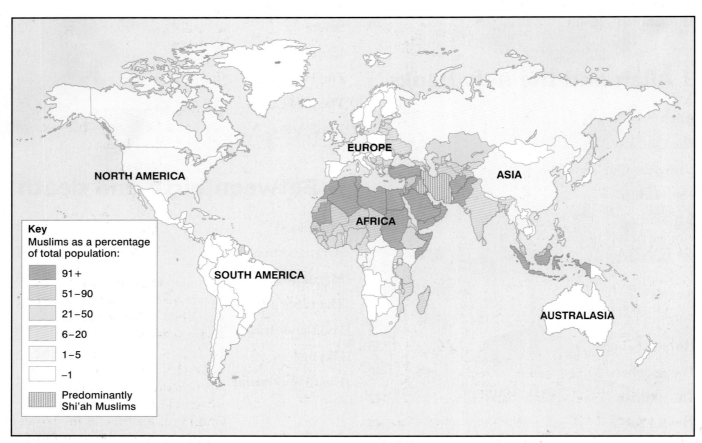

Key
Muslims as a percentage of total population:

- 91+
- 51–90
- 21–50
- 6–20
- 1–5
- –1
- Predominantly Shi'ah Muslims

With the help of an atlas, make a list of ten countries where more than half the population is Muslim.

Allah (the Arabic name for God) and that Muhammad is His messenger. This statement of faith is known as the Shahadah. It is the basic belief of all Muslims.

Islam and Muslims

The word Islam can carry more than one meaning. It can mean 'submission to God' – a Muslim entrusts himself completely to God and dedicates himself or herself to Him. It can also mean 'peace' – the Prophet Muhammad said that a good Muslim is one who helps to spread peace and who is kind to orphans. In the Qur'an Muslims are called a community of the 'middle path'. They should avoid extremes and encourage each other to do good. Together with people of other communities, they should work together for the good of all people.

Islam is also an inner struggle which each believer wages. It is the struggle to live life to the full, to rise above its attractions and to dedicate oneself to God. Such dedication requires regular worship, but this alone is not enough. A person must also try to do their best for their family, for orphans, for the needy and sick. They must try to be tolerant and forgiving too.

This is the city of Makkah, one of the the most important cities on earth for all Muslims. What five things can you find out about this city?

- Who is Allah?
- Who was the last of the prophets?
- What is the Qur'an?

1 In your own words, write a sentence to explain the meaning of each of these words:
a Allah.
b Islam.
c Muslim.
d Prophet.

2 This is the symbol of slam. It is found in many different places in the Muslim community.

a Copy the symbol into your exercise book and describe the two parts of the symbol underneath your drawing.

b Why is this an appropriate symbol for Islam? [Clue: Early Muslims who lived in the desert used the stars for finding direction and the moon for determining the months of their calendar.]

Sunni and Shi'ah Muslims

Muslims understand Islam in different ways because people have various abilities and temperaments. They are also influenced by what other people say and by their own surroundings. The Muslim community itself became richer when people from other cultures accepted Islam.

When the Prophet Muhammad was alive, Muslims would go to him if they had a question to ask or a difference of opinion. When he died, Muslims could not agree on a leader to succeed him. Their disagreement led to a division in the community. Islam divided into two main branches known as Sunni and Shi'ah.

Sunni Muslims

Some Muslims believed that the Prophet had not appointed anyone to succeed him as leader. Eventually, these Muslims came together and became known as Sunnis. The word Sunni means 'people who follow the sunnah of the Prophet' (i.e. his example in what he said and did). Sunnis believed that the Qur'an and the sunnah were enough to guide Muslims, and that the Prophet's example added to an understanding of the Qur'an.

The Sunnis relied on the learned members, or ulama, of the community to produce rules of conduct by studying the Qur'an and the **Hadith**. The ulama also used their judgement, local customs and agreements among themselves to help produce the rules.

The Sunnis agreed that the Muslims must have a leader. He was known as the caliph and was elected by important members of the community. His main task was to maintain law and order so that people could follow their religion and live their lives in peace. The first caliph was Abu Bakr, a much respected companion of the Prophet. The Sunnis are, by far, the largest branch of Islam. Nine out of every ten Muslims are Sunnis.

Shi'ah Muslims

Other groups of Muslims believed that the Prophet had already named his successor. He was **Ali**, the Prophet's cousin and son-in-law, who was married to Fatima, the Prophet's daughter. These groups were known as the Shi'ah of Ali, or the party of Ali. They believed that the Prophet had said that Muslims should follow not only the Qur'an but also a leader chosen from the Prophet's own family.

Ali was their first leader, or **imam**. They supported the claim of Ali that the leadership

What did Sunni Muslims rely on the ulama for?

Ali kisses the hand of the Prophet Muhammad. Who was Ali?

For your dictionary

Ali was the cousin and son-in-law of Muhammad. He became the fourth caliph of the Sunni Muslims, and was the first imam of the Shi'ah Muslims.
The **Hadith** are the sayings and traditions of the Prophet Muhammad.
Imam is the title given to the leader of the Shi'ah Muslims. An iman is also the person who leads communal prayer.

- Into which two main branches is Islam divided?
- Which group of people produced rules of conduct for Sunni Muslims by studying the Qur'an and the Hadith?
- What is one difference between Sunni and Shi'ah Muslims?

belonged to him and his descendants through Fatima. The Shi'ah believe in a line of leaders from the family of the Prophet and Ali. They follow the sunnah of the Prophet, which they learn from their imams. They also follow the traditions of their imams.

Although Ali claimed that he was the imam, he co-operated with Abu Bakr and the two caliphs after him. He also praised the conduct of Abu Bakr and the second caliph, Umar, for what they had done for Islam. Sunni Muslims also respect Ali as the fourth caliph.

One religion

Sunni and Shi'ah Muslims belong to the one religion of Islam. They all agree on the Shahadah. They follow the sunnah of the Prophet Muhammad and believe that he was the final prophet. They share the same principles of belief and behaviour. They believe that Muslims should act with peace and responsibility. Yet they may understand what this involves differently. Sunni Muslims may look to their ulama whilst Shi'ahs rely on the guidance of their imams.

Copy these sentences into your book and fill in the missing words as you go.

a   The word _____ means the example of the Prophet Muhammad.

b   _____ believe that the _____ and the sunnah are sufficient to guide all Muslims.

c   The leader of the Sunni Muslim community was known as the _____.

d   The first _____ was _____ _____, who was a respected friend of Muhammad, the _____.

e   _____ Muslims believe that Muhammad chose the person to succeed him. He was _____, who was the _____ of Muhammad.

f   Shi'ah Muslims follow the traditions of their _____.

The spiritual side of Islam

An important part of Islam is its mystical side. Many Shi'ah and Sunni Muslims believe in mystical Islam. They are known as **sufis**. To be 'mystical' is to believe that your inner, or spiritual, life is very important. While a person should live well he or she should not forget that their soul is the most important part of them.

For which spiritual truths might this Sufi be searching?

In every religious action sufis try to understand its deeper, inner meaning. For example, they believe that to **fast** is not only to stop eating and drinking. A person must fast with all of their senses. They must not think, hear, see or do evil things. Sufis do not stop at praying five times a day. They often pray more frequently at special gatherings, as the frequent remembrance of God brings the soul closer to Him.

Sufis search for the hidden, spiritual truths behind outward things. For example, some sufis say that every sound in nature is a sign of the unity of God. Everything in nature, like a person's own soul, is a reminder that God is everywhere:

'We shall show them our signs in the horizons and in themselves, till it is clear to them that it is the truth.' (Surah 41:53)

Muslims believe that they must do certain things as part of their religious duty. This includes praying regularly, fasting during the month of **Ramadan** and setting aside a portion of money to help others. They are part of **din** and are done for the good of a person's soul.

Living in the world

Like everyone else, a Muslim must work to earn a decent living and strive to be on good terms with other people. Muslims must spend time learning how to be a decent citizen. Whilst these matters have to do with the world they are not different from the spiritual side of life. Everything

that Muslims do is guided by Islam. They are taught to think before doing anything, to work out what is right and to see how their actions will affect others. Every thought and action has a witness, whether the Muslim is alone or with other people. That witness is God and nothing can be hidden from Him.

However busy a Muslim is, he or she will always find a few moments to remember God. That is why Muslims describe Islam as a way of life. It brings together the spiritual and everyday aspects of life.

The Qur'an tells all followers of Islam to:

'Serve God, and join not any partners with Him;
And do good –
To parents, kinsfolk, orphans, those in need,
Neighbours who are near,
Neighbours who are strangers,
The Companion by your side,
The way-farer (ye meet),
And what your right hands possess...' (Surah 4:36)

Why do you think that fasting is an important spiritual exercise?

- What is a sufi?
- What is fasting and how might a sufi understand the word?
- How is a Muslim taught to live in the world?

For your dictionary

Din is the way of life i.e. religion together with its practices.
To **fast** is to go without food or drink.
Ramadan is the ninth month of the Muslim calendar in which Muslims must fast during daylight hours.
Sufis are Muslims who seek a close, direct and personal experience of God.

What do you think the Qur'an means by the following:
a 'Serve God, and join not any partners with Him.'
b 'Neighbours who are near, Neighbours who are strangers.'
c 'The Companion by your side.'

What is a Muslim?

The Muslim community throughout the world is made up of many different groups and traditions. Each of them has its own distinctive way of life. Muslims use the Qur'an and the Hadith as their most important sources of inspiration. They also share many basic beliefs and teachings.

The teachings of Islam

These are some of the most important teachings of Islam. They will be explained further at later stages throughout this book.

- There is only one God – Allah – who has created all things. He guides those who submit to him in the right path.

- Muhammad was the last, and greatest, of God's prophets. He received the final, complete revelation from Allah through the **Angel Jibril**. There have been many other prophets sent to each community to bring God's message in a language that they could understand.

- The Qur'an contains Allah's final message to humankind, as revealed to Muhammad. It contains moral and spiritual guidance for all Muslims.

- The Qur'an refers to the Day of Judgement when Allah will judge every man and every woman on their deeds. It urges people to lead upright lives and to seek to do good to others.

This is an eighteenth-century Qur'an. What is the Qur'an?

Being a Muslim

The Qur'an guides believers to reflect on their actions. It places upon each Muslim the duty of doing good and avoiding evil. Muslims are encouraged to be kind and generous to everyone. They are made aware of their responsibilities towards the poor and the weak, the aged and the lonely.

Muslim history reveals examples of people who set a high moral standard for themselves. Muslims are inspired by the mission of the Prophet Muhammad, the sacrifices made by members of his family and the struggle of early Muslims to fight injustice and oppression.

- Why is Muhammad very important for all Muslims?
- Where are the revelations of Allah to Muhammad brought together?
- What is the Day of Judgement?

What responsibilities do Muslims have towards the vulnerable?

For your dictionary

The **Angel Jibril** (Gabriel) is a very important angel who delivered Allah's message to the prophets.

Look back

Hadith (page 7)

Complete the following sentences by matching the beginnings on the left with the correct ending from the list on the right.

The Qur'an guides believers	the last, and greatest, of all the prophets.
The Prophet Muhammad was	Allah's final message.
Muhammad received Allah's word through	to bring God's message.
The Qur'an contains	to reflect on their actions.
On the Day of Judgement	the Angel Jibril.
The prophets were sent	every man and woman will be judged.

The early years of Muhammad

Muhammad was born in the city of Makkah in about 570 CE. At that time, the city was at the centre of a very prosperous caravan trade between Arabia and the Mediterranean Sea. The people who lived there thought it was a holy city. They worshipped many different gods.

The early life of Muhammad

Muhammad never knew his father. He died before the boy was born. When he was just six years old his mother also died. His grandfather, who had then taken care of him, died two years after that. An orphan at an early age, Muhammad was looked after by his uncle, Abu Talib.

Muhammad worked as a camel driver and then as a trader. He soon built up a reputation as an honest man. His honesty earned him the nickname 'Al-Amin' – 'The Trustworthy One'.

How did other people regard the young Muhammad when he worked on a camel train?

Gulf of Oman

Arabian Sea

• Madinah

• Makkah

Red Sea

0   1200
km

In which country are the important cities of Makkah and **Madinah** now situated?

What is the Ka'bah?

Muhammad soon started to work for **Khadijah**, who owned one of the camel trains. She was a rich widow who was pleased with Muhammad's work. Although she was 15 years older than him, Khadijah asked Muhammad to marry her. They had six children – four daughters and two sons. The two boys died when they were young.

In Makkah

Muhammad was a very religious man. He spent a long time praying in the desert around Makkah.

He was deeply troubled by the way that the people lived in the town. They worshipped many idols, which were made of stone, wood or clay and kept in or around the **Ka'bah**. The Ka'bah stood in the centre of Makkah, as it still does today. You can see it surrounded by pilgrims in the photograph opposite. Muslims believe that the Ka'bah was built originally by Ibrahim (Abraham), a prophet who lived about 4,000 years ago.

One day heavy rain damaged the walls of the Ka'bah. Many people repaired them, but they then fell out over who should put the **Black Stone** back in place – to be chosen was a great honour.

As they could not agree, they decided that the first person to walk through the city gates the next morning would make the decision. That person was Muhammad. He decided to lay a cloak on the ground and the Black Stone was placed on it. The four leaders of the tribes each took a corner, and Muhammad guided the Black Stone back into position.

- What is the Ka'bah?
- Who was Khadijah?
- What is the Black Stone?

1 Copy this paragraph into your exercise book and fill in the missing words as you go.

The _____ dominates the centre of the city of _____.

_____ believe that the _____, a shrine, was built by

_____, who was one of the early _____, about

_____ years ago. The _____ _____ is in the corner

of the _____. _____ believe that this came down from

_____.

2 Answer each of these questions in your own words:

a Why did Muhammad have a sad childhood?
b What do you think about Muhammad's solution for replacing the Black Stone?

For your dictionary

The **Black Stone** is an oval stone set in the corner of the Ka'bah. It is believed to have come down from Allah to Ibrahim and his son, Isma'il.

The **Ka'bah** ('cube') is the shrine in Makkah that is set in the courtyard of the Great Mosque.

Khadijah was the wealthy widow who employed Muhammad to lead her caravans. She later became his wife.

Madinah is the city that welcomed Muhammad in 622 CE after he left Makkah. Muhammad is buried in Madinah.

The Night of Power

Every day, Muhammad prayed in a cave just outside Makkah. This cave, at Mount Hira, is still there today. Muhammad saw the rich and powerful mistreating the poor, the weak and those without protection. He could not believe that such activities pleased Allah.

What do you think Muhammad learned in the time he spent praying to God in this cave?

The Angel Jibril

One day, something quite amazing happened to Muhammad. It changed his life completely. In the silence of the cave, he heard the voice of the Angel Jibril commanding him to recite (speak out loud) the first verses of God's revelation.

When Muhammad went outside the cave, he heard a voice saying, 'O Muhammad! You are the messenger of God and I am Jibril.' Muhammad saw an angel whose wings spread from horizon to horizon. This image of the angel conveys the idea that angels are spiritual beings, unlike creatures of the earth.

Muhammad went home quickly. He told his wife, Khadijah, what had happened. She assured him that the vision had come from Allah. Khadijah, Ali (the Prophet's cousin) and **Abu Bakr** became the first converts to Islam.

Further visions

For some time, Muhammad had no further visions. Then the angel came once more and revealed the following verses to him:

'By the morning hours, and by the night when it is most still, your Lord has not left you... Did He not find you an orphan and protect you? Did He not find you lost and guide you? Did He not find you poor and enrich you?' (Surah 93:1–8)

Upon receiving these verses, Muhammad knew that God would never abandon him. God would guide him in his mission as the final messenger and prophet.

- What happened to change Muhammad's life completely?
- Who became Muhammad's first companions and what did they do?
- How did Muhammad receive the messages of the Qur'an?

The people of Makkah worshipped the sun, the moon, the stars and stone pillars. They made idols of them and put them in the Ka'bah. Why do you think the people worshipped these objects?

1 The first verses that Allah revealed to Muhammad are given in Chapter 96 of the Qur'an:

'In the Name of God, the Compassionate, the Merciful. Recite: In the Name of your Lord who created man from a clot of blood. Recite: And your Lord is Most Bountiful, who taught by the pen, taught man that which he did not know.' (Surah 96:1–5)

a Three names are given to God here. What do they each mean?

b What has God done to, and for, humankind?

2 **a** How do you think Muhammad might have felt when he began to receive visions of the Angel Jibril? How would you have felt?

b How do you think Khadijah might have felt when her husband told her that he was receiving visions of the Angel Jibril? How would you have felt in her place?

c How do you think Muhammad might have felt when Khadijah told him that she believed in him, and became his first convert? How would you have felt in his place?

For your dictionary

Abu Bakr was a close companion of Muhammad who became the first caliph after Muhammad's death.

Look back

Ali (page 7)
Angel Jibril (page 11)
Ka'bah (page 13)
Khadijah (page 13)

The Night Journey

In 619 CE two events greatly upset Muhammad. First his wife and then his uncle, Abu Talib, died. Abu Talib had looked after Muhammad since childhood. Muhammad was very sad.

The enemies of Muhammad had made his life a misery in Makkah. He was wondering what the future held when he had an amazing experience. It is called the **Mi'raj**. Muslims call this experience the 'Night Journey' of Muhammad.

The Night Journey

One night, Muhammad was sleeping by the Ka'bah. The Angel Jibril came to him, woke him up, and took him to **Jerusalem** on a strange animal that looked like a horse with wings. Its name was **Buraq**. From Jerusalem, Muhammad was taken up to heaven. All of the earlier prophets were there and Muhammad spoke to them. The angel then took Muhammad higher and higher into the heavens. He saw the throne of Allah in the distance. Peace and pure light surrounded him. Muhammad felt the presence of Allah.

Suddenly, the experience came to an end and Muhammad was taken back to earth. The place where he had been asleep was still warm. Water was still trickling out of a cup that he had knocked over. The experience had taken place in a split second of time.

The story about the Mi'raj was told by Muhammad to his companions. Since then, Muslims have wondered about its meaning. Some have thought that Muhammad's Night Journey was a physical one. Others believe that it was a mystical experience with a deeper meaning. For example, Buraq was not really a physical horse but stood for the idea of spiritual progress. Whatever its meaning, its effect upon Muhammad was very deep and remained with him for the rest of his life. He was shortly to become a fearless leader. Soon many converts were added to Islam in both Makkah and Madinah.

What was Buraq and what was unusual about it?

- Which two events in 619 CE had such a great effect upon Muhammad?
- What was the Mi'raj?
- Where was Muhammad taken during the Night Journey, and what happened there?

Why is the Dome of the Rock mosque so important to Muslims?

1 These words are found in the Qur'an:

'God is the Light of the heavens and of the earth. The example of His Light is as a niche in which is a lamp. The lamp is in the glass. The glass is as it were a shining star... Light upon Light. God guides to His Light whom He will. And Allah speaks to mankind in allegories, for Allah is Knower of all things.' (Surah 24:35)

a Why do you think the Night Journey was so important in the life of Muhammad?

b What do you think Muhammad discovered about Allah on the Night Journey?

2 The **mosque** of the Dome of the Rock is one of the most important buildings in Islam.

a Where does the mosque stand?

b What is the link between this mosque and the Night Journey?

For your dictionary

Buraq was the winged horse that took Muhammad to heaven. Its name means 'lightning'.

Jerusalem is the city that contains the Dome of the Rock mosque. Muhammad ascended to heaven from the site of this mosque. The city is sacred to Muslims, Jews and Christians.

The **Mi'raj** is the Night Journey that Muhammad made to heaven. The word means 'ladder' or 'ascent'.

A **mosque** is a Muslim place of public worship and gathering. Muslims also have other places of prayer and gathering in different parts of the world, which are known by different names.

 Look back

Angel Jibril (page 11)
Madinah (page 13)

The Hijrah

The revelation of God's messages and the Night Journey were important events in the life of Muhammad. The journey which took the Prophet from Makkah to Madinah in 622 CE was important also. This journey, the **Hijrah**, is the event from which all Muslims date their calendar. Everything after 622 CE is dated AH – 'After Hijrah'.

After returning from the Night Journey, Muhammad once again preached to the people in Makkah. One day, some pilgrims from **Yathrib** made a journey to the Ka'bah. They heard Muhammad preaching and invited him to their home town.

Travelling to Yathrib

After Muhammad had agreed to go, he sent some friends on ahead while he stayed in Makkah. His friends were frightened that he would be attacked on the way – a journey of over 400 km. Muhammad waited for the final word from Allah to say that he should leave. Finally, he left Makkah in the middle of the night. On the way, he hid in a cave for four days as his enemies gave chase from Makkah. At one point, they stood right outside the cave. However, Allah had made a spider weave a web across the cave's entrance and a pigeon build its nest there, so his enemies suspected nothing and Muhammad was safe.

Reaching Yathrib

When Muhammad arrived in the city, everyone wanted him to live with them. The Prophet did not want to upset anyone, so he said that his camel would make the final decision. The camel knelt down at the place where dates were laid out to dry. Muhammad bought the land and built his house there. Part of the house became the first mosque. Muhammad soon became the ruler of Yathrib – or Madinah as it was renamed when Muhammad arrived.

Muhammad's new rules

There were many different groups in the city. Muhammad said that all people should be treated equally. He asked the Muslims to act with unity and dignity, to pray regularly, to fast during the month of Ramadan, to give money to the poor and to treat slaves with kindness. To set an example, Muhammad chose **Bilal**, a former slave, to call the Muslims to prayer.

Why did Muhammad's enemies not suspect that he was hiding in the cave?

- Why did Muhammad decide to go to Yathrib, and what did the name of this city later become?
- What was the Hijrah?
- What new rules did Muhammad introduce for the people of Madinah?

1 Look at the picture above. What problems do you think Muhammad faced as he travelled from Makkah to Yathrib?

2 Why do you think that:

a Muslims date their calendar from the Hijrah?

b Muhammad fell out with some of the people in Madinah when he began to introduce new rules in the city?

3 Muhammad taught Muslims about the importance of the belief in one God and in following His guidance. He also taught them to attend to both their religious and worldly duties equally.

a Give some examples of how a Muslim family might lead a balanced life today.

b Why do you think family life is so important to Muslims?

For your dictionary

Bilal was the slave from Abyssinia (now called Ethiopia) who became one of Muhammad's companions. He was the first person to issue the call to prayer.

The **Hijrah** was the journey made by Muhammad from Makkah to Yathrib in 622 CE. The word means 'migration' or 'departure'.

Yathrib was the town that welcomed Muhammad and his companions after they left Makkah. After Muhammad's arrival, it became known as Madinah.

 Look back

Ka'bah (page 13)
Madinah (page 13)
Mosque (page 17)

19

Muḥammad in Madinah

Most of the people in Madinah accepted Muhammad as their prophet and leader, and he could have chosen to live like a king. Instead, he continued to live like an ordinary man, helping his family with everyday chores.

In Muhammad's time, trade had created a wide gap between the rich and the poor. He stressed that all people were equal regardless of their wealth, religion or race. He also stressed that orphans, widows and slaves should be given protection and shelter. He told the people that he was not the ruler of the city: Allah was. Everything in the world belonged to Him.

A just society

Conflicts between tribes were common, but Muhammad told the people to unite as one community for the good of all. He encouraged forgiveness and tolerance, rather than revenge. Muhammad also arranged for a part of all the community's wealth to be given to the needy.

Before Muhammad's arrival in Madinah, the Arab society had been based on tribal customs. Honour and pride in one's wealth and strength were the most important things. Muhammad led the people to a way of life that called for generosity, modesty and self-sacrifice.

Changing attitudes

Muhammad also tried to change the attitudes of Muslims to some important issues of the time.

- Although he did not approve of slavery, Muhammad thought that it was necessary at the time. The families provided protection for the slaves, who would otherwise have had to fend for themselves. Muhammad advised his people to improve the conditions of the slaves, and to free a slave was an act of great kindness and generosity.

- In many societies of the past, women were treated unfairly. A man could marry several wives and easily disown them if he chose. Muhammad improved the position of women by insisting that they be treated with respect and dignity. He allowed women to own property and engage in their own businesses.

Do you think that the guidelines which Muhammad introduced in Madinah could be used successfully today?

- Who was the real ruler of Madinah whilst Muhammad was its governor?
- Why did Muhammad accept slavery although he did not approve of it?
- How did Muhammad set out to improve the way that women were treated?

1 Bilal was a slave from another country. He was the first person selected by Muhammad to work within the Muslim community. His job was to call the faithful to prayer. This is a very important post. What point do you think Muhammad was making by appointing Bilal?

2 Muhammad introduced many new laws into Madinah. Can you suggest why he:

a discouraged the drinking of alcohol and gambling in the city?

b insisted that workers were paid their wages as soon as they had earned them?

c banned all forms of cruelty to animals?

d insisted that everyone spent time feeding the needy?

e told people not to talk about others behind their backs?

Look back

Bilal (page 19)
Madinah (page 13)

Muhammad conquers Makkah

Muhammad had begun to create a new community in Madinah. This community was based on fairness and justice. However, the Makkans were determined to destroy all that Muhammad had achieved and to return to their old way of life.

Battles

A number of battles were fought between the armies of Makkah and Madinah. In one of them, the Battle of Badr, 314 of Muhammad's companions were able to defeat 1,000 men from Makkah. This convinced the Muslims that Allah was with them.

The people of Makkah were thirsty for revenge. In 625 CE, a large army of them attacked the Muslims at Mount Uhud. The Muslims lost the fight and Muhammad began to wonder whether Allah had deserted him.

What do you think the Muslims might have learned from their defeat on Mount Uhud?

The Muslims learned a lot from this setback. They knew that Allah had been testing their faith. They also became aware that they needed a greater unity amongst themselves. They made up their minds to fight against the Makkans until they were victorious.

The defeat of Makkah

In 630 CE, Muhammad marched to Makkah. This time no one could stand in his way. Once in Makkah he marched seven times around the Ka'bah and kissed the Black Stone. He then called everyone to attend midday prayers.

Muhammad then turned his attention to the Ka'bah. He threw out all of the idols and ordered that all pictures in the shrine be removed. The only pictures allowed to be left were those of Maryam (Mary) and Isa (Jesus). He had conquered the city in the name of Allah.

Soon, many people in Makkah accepted Islam. Muhammad forgave his old enemies – those who had waged war with him for many years. Over time, Islam became the faith of many people in Arabia and the surrounding lands.

How do you think that Muhammad's victory over the people of Makkah proved that Allah was with him?

- What did Muhammad come to believe after the Battle of Badr?
- What happened at Mount Uhud?
- What did Muhammad do after he entered the city of Makkah in triumph?

1 The Qur'an explains why the Muslims lost the battle on Mount Uhud:

'He [God] allowed you to be defeated in order to test you. But now He has forgiven you, for God is gracious to the faithful.' (Surah 3:152)

a On a human level, why did the Muslim army fail to defeat the people of Makkah on Mount Uhud?

b Why did Allah allow the Muslims to be defeated on Mount Uhud?

2 What did the Muslims learn from their defeat on Mount Uhud?

Look back

Black Stone (page 13)
Ka'bah (page 13)
Madinah (page 13)

Muhammad's death

By 632 CE, Muhammad was aware that his life was coming to an end. He wanted to make one last journey from Madinah to Makkah. He went with 150,000 pilgrims. Climbing with them up to the **Mount of Mercy**, he was able to deliver one last sermon.

The last sermon

Muhammad told everyone to listen carefully to what he had to say, as he did not think he would make another pilgrimage. Muhammad told them how they should live as Muslims. Everyone must:

- live in peace with each other.
- respect the rights and property of each other.
- put any hatred and cruelty to one side.
- look after their own families.
- respect the women and treat them with fairness.

Muhammad told them that he had left them two important things. Sunni Muslims believe that these two things were the Qur'an and Muhammad's own example. Sunni Muslims do not believe that Muhammad appointed his successor. Shi'ah Muslims believe that the two things left by Muhammad were the Qur'an and his family. They claim that Muhammad appointed his cousin and son-in-law, Ali, to be his successor at a place called Ghadir Khumm. Ali is the first imam of the Shi'ah Muslims.

The death of Muhammad

Soon after Muhammad returned from Makkah, his health began to give way and he fell ill with a severe fever. He tried to reach the place of prayer each day but he grew weaker. He asked his friend, Abu Bakr, to lead the prayers for him instead.

Muhammad died on 8 June 632 CE. He was buried the following day in the house he had built himself. Abu Bakr announced to the waiting crowd that the Prophet was dead. He told them:

'Those of you who worshipped Muhammad know that Muhammad is dead. As for those of you who worship God, God is living and will never die.'

He then quoted a verse from the Qur'an:

'Muhammad is no more than an apostle [messenger]: other apostles have passed away before him. If he die… will you recant [give up]? (Surah 3:144)

What did Muhammad tell his fellow pilgrims on the Mount of Mercy?

This mosque in Madinah is built on the traditional burial-place of Muhammad. What did Abu Bakr do after Muhammad's death?

1 These are the last things Muhammad said in his sermon:

'Listen to me very carefully. Worship God, be steadfast in prayer, fast during Ramadan, pay alms [money] to the less fortunate. People, no prophet or messenger will come after me, and no new faith will emerge. All those who listen to me will pass on my words to others, and those to others again.'

a Muhammad told his followers to do four things. What were they?

b What do you think Muhammad meant when he said, '...no prophet or messenger will come after me, and no new faith will emerge'?

c What will those who hear the words of Muhammad do?

2 Look again at the words that Abu Bakr spoke after the death of Muhammad.

a What do you think he was trying to tell the people when he said that Muhammad was dead and only Allah was alive for evermore?

b What does the Qur'an mean when it says that Muhammad was just a prophet and other prophets had died before him?

c What do you think the Qur'an means by the words, 'will you recant'?

- What did Muhammad do on the Mount of Mercy?
- Why was Muhammad's last pilgrimage so important?
- What did Abu Bakr tell the people after Muhammad's death?

For your dictionary

The **Mount of Mercy** is the hill from which Muhammad gave his farewell sermon.

 Look back

Abu Bakr (page 15)
Ali (page 7)
Fast (page 9)
Iman (page 7)
Madinah (page 13)

Allah and the holy books
Allah

There is one belief in Islam that is more important than any other – there is one God, Allah, and Muhammad is His messenger. The name 'Allah' means 'the God'. Allah has spoken to the world through His prophets. The last, and greatest, of these was Muhammad.

The Qur'an asks believers to remember Allah through His Beautiful Names. According to a Hadith of the Prophet, there are 99 Beautiful Names of Allah. A Muslim is able to call on any of these names, night or day. In the words of the Qur'an:

'The most beautiful names belong to God: so call on Him by them.'

Why do you think tasbih are useful?

These names are repeated continually throughout the day. To help a Muslim, there are special beads called **tasbih** which can be used. You will find out more about these on pages 68 and 69.

Allah is One

Muslims believe that Allah is One. This belief is called **Tawhid**. This means that Allah is beyond all human understanding and cannot be compared to anything else. He is unique, He knows everything, sees everything and can do anything. The Qur'an says:

'No mortal eyes can see Him, though He sees all eyes. He is the All-Subtle, the All-Aware.' (Surah 6:103)

Allah is the creator of everything that exists. Nothing can exist unless Allah has made it. Because He has made all things, He is also the judge of everything. He is all-powerful. Yet He is also full of mercy to all who submit to Him.

God and the world

All men and women depend entirely on God. They owe their beginning in the womb to Him. They continue to exist because of His mercy. They only draw breath because Allah allows it. The moment that permission is withdrawn the person dies. This is why everybody owes it to Allah to submit to Him.

Who has created everything that exists?

- What is the most important belief in Islam?
- What does the Qur'an say about the different names of Allah?
- What is Tawhid?

What will this young child be told about God as she grows up?

 There is a beautiful Muslim legend which explains why Allah has 99 and not 100 names. According to the legend, there is one more name for Allah but this is only known to the camel, and the camel is not telling! Behind this legend there is an important spiritual truth. What do you think it is?

 Amongst other names, Allah is called the Compassionate, the Merciful, the Forgiver and the Wise.

a Find out some of the other names of Allah.

b Are there any names on the list which surprise you? If so, can you explain why?

c Make a list of the names given to God in one other religion that you know about. Are there any names which are similar or the same as those in Islam?

For your dictionary

A **tasbih** is a set of 99 prayer beads, used by Muslims to help them to remember the names of Allah.
Tawhid is the Muslim belief that God is One.

Look back

Hadith (page 7)

The Qur'an

Muslims love and respect their holy book very highly. It is called the Qur'an. The word itself means 'recitation' and this is important in two ways:

- The words of the Qur'an were originally recited (read aloud) to Muhammad by the Angel Jibril.
- The beauty of the Qur'an is only fully appreciated when it is read out loud. Reading the Qur'an aloud is a central part of every act of Muslim worship.

The Qur'an, revealed in Arabic, is the word of Allah. The essence of the Qur'an is eternal. It was revealed to Muhammad through the Angel Jibril. The original Qur'an is preserved in heaven. When the Angel Jibril spoke to Muhammad, he was reading from the heavenly copy. This means that the Qur'an carries Allah's full authority.

In what language is the Qur'an written?

The surahs

There are 114 chapters in the Qur'an. They are called **surahs**. All of them, except one, begin with the words:

'In the Name of God, the Compassionate, the Merciful.'

Each of the surahs come from Allah. They could not be created by human hands.

The surahs are not written down in the order in which they were revealed to Muhammad. They are arranged in the order in which they were collected by Muhammad's companions. Within 20 years of Muhammad's death, the Qur'an existed as one book.

Each surah has its own title. The titles come from some word or subject in that chapter. So, for example, the second surah is called 'The Cow' because it contains a story about Musa (Moses) asking the people to sacrifice a cow.

The surah which Muslims know best is the first. They recite it every day. You can read this surah on the opposite page.

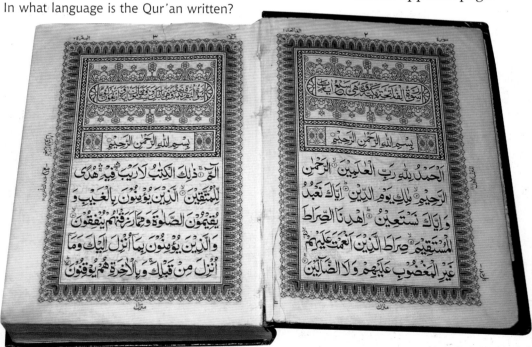

- Why is the Qur'an special?
- What is a surah?
- What is in the Qur'an?

The teachings of the Qur'an

The teachings of the Qur'an guide every Muslim. They tell them how to live day by day as they submit themselves to Allah. They also explain how they can prepare themselves for the Day of Judgement. For example, it tells them:

- to share their wealth and knowledge.

- to treat every human being with respect.

- to look after widows, orphans and the sick.

- not to engage in any activities, such as drinking alcohol or taking drugs, which will damage the mind.

- to help pay the debts of the poor and free the slaves.

The Qur'an contains stories about the many great prophets of the past, including Ibrahim (Abraham), Yusuf (Joseph), Isa (Jesus) and Musa (Moses).

Why do you think children and young people are taught to understand the message of the Qur'an?

1 Copy out these sentences and fill in the missing words as you go:

a The Qur'an is the word of _____ and was transmitted to _____ by the _____ _____.

b Each _____ in the _____ begins with the words 'In the Name of _____, the _____, the _____.'

c The Qur'an contains stories about many great _____ of the past, including _____, _____, _____ and _____.

2 This is the opening surah of the Qur'an:

'Praise be to God, Lord of the Universe,

The Compassionate, the Merciful,

Sovereign of the Day of Judgement!

You alone we worship, and to You alone we turn for help.

Guide us to the straight path,

The path of those whom You have favoured,

Not of those who have incurred Your wrath [made you angry],

Nor of those who have gone astray. (Surah 1)

a Several titles and names are given to Allah in this extract. Make a list of them.

b What does each worshipper ask Allah to do for them?

For your dictionary

A **surah** is a chapter in the Qur'an.

Look back

Angel Jibril (page 11)

Using the Qur'an

The Prophet Muhammad said this about the Qur'an:

'The best of you is he who has learnt the Qur'an and then taught it.'

Muslims make every effort to learn and understand Allah's message in the Qur'an. Many of them also teach the holy book to others.

Muslim schools

Every mosque has its own school, or **madrasah**, in which young Muslims learn about their faith. In Britain, they usually go straight to this school after their day school. They then learn about Islam for a few hours each day.

Both boys and girls start their religious education at an early age. They are encouraged to continue with this education when they become teenagers. Many of them continue with this learning and become teachers themselves.

Learning the Qur'an

The vast majority of Muslims are not Arabs and do not speak Arabic. Therefore, they read the Qur'an as it is translated into their own language. Although the Qur'an has been translated into many languages, it always loses something when it is translated out of Arabic. Muslims therefore try to understand the meaning and spirit of Allah's revelation.

Why do all Muslim children learn to speak and read Arabic?

Friday prayers

Every Friday, Muslims gather in their mosque for prayers. This is the most important act of Muslim worship. It takes place at midday. Before the prayers begin, the imam gives a short talk. This is called the **khutbah**. The imam is a leader of the prayers in a mosque. For Shi'ah Muslims, the imam is the spiritual leader of the community. The imam who leads the prayers must:

- have a good understanding of Islam.
- carry the respect of his fellow Muslims.
- be known for his own holiness and that of his family.
- have studied both the Qur'an and the Hadith.

In the khutbah, the imam explains a passage from the Qur'an or a story about the Prophet Muhammad.

The Qur'an is highly respected. No one can talk, eat, drink or make a noise while it is being read in public. When it is not being used, the holy book must be kept covered and placed up high in the room. It must never touch the ground.

Why is the Qur'an often placed on a stool when it is not being used?

- What is a madrasah and why do children go there?
- What is the khutbah?
- What kind of person must an imam be?

1 These three quotations come from the Qur'an. They tell Muslims how they should treat their holy book:

'He [Allah] has revealed to you the Book with the Truth...' (Surah 3:2)

'This Qur'an could not have been devised by any but God.' (Surah 10:38)

'This [Qur'an] is insight from your Lord, and a guidance and a mercy for people that believe. And when the Qur'an is recited, listen to it with attention.' (Surah 7:203–4)

Use these quotations to help you answer these questions:

a Who has given the Qur'an to mankind?
b What is 'the Book'?
c Where has the Qur'an come from?
d Could the Qur'an have been written by human beings?
e Who is able to know the true origin of the Qur'an?

2 Write down three ways in which Muslim and non-Muslim educations are similar or different.

For your dictionary

The **khutbah** is the sermon delivered by the imam in Friday prayers.

A **madrasah** is a school in a mosque where young Muslims study Islam.

Look back

Hadith (page 7)
Iman (page 7)
Mosque (page 17)

The Hadith

The Qur'an occupies a central place in Islam. However, the Hadith are also very important. These are the recorded words or sayings of Muhammad himself. Because he was the ideal Muslim, his life is a good example to others. The Hadith are respected very highly, but they are not included in the Qur'an.

Muhammad could not read or write, so many reliable people wrote down his sayings and teachings. Others were passed on from person to person by word of mouth.

An unbroken chain

After Muhammad's death, an enormous collection of these sayings built up. The genuine Hadith had to be sorted out from those that were false, so a rule was introduced. A genuine Hadith must include the name of every human link between the writer and the Prophet.

You can see how this worked in the following extract. It comes from one of the collections of Hadith which was put together in the ninth century – well after the death of the Prophet. It says:

'Abdallah Ibn-Awad told me: Al Fadl Ibn-Ata told us: Isma'il Ibn-Sayfi told us on the authority of Yahya Ibn-Abdallah Ibn-Sayfi that he heard Abu Ma'bad, the freedman of Ibn-Abbas say, "I heard Ibn-Abbas say, 'When the Prophet, the blessings of Allah be on him and peace, sent Mu'adh to the Yemen, he said to him...'"'

Shi'ah Muslims rely on Hadith reported from members of the Prophet's family, and most importantly from their imams.

This woman is reading the Hadith. What does it contain?

Why are the Hadith important?

The Hadith do not carry the same authority as the Qur'an. That book is Allah's eternal record and preserved in heaven. However, because the words are Muhammad's, the Hadith are open to discussion. Those in the Qur'an are not.

The Hadith cover almost any situation that a Muslim might have to face. One part covers questions arising from belief and worship. The other covers matters to do with everyday life.

- How did the Hadith come into being?
- What rule was introduced to distinguish between true and false Hadith?
- How are the Hadith different from the Qur'an?

How might a Muslim make use of the Hadith?

1 This Hadith was recorded by Abu Dharr:

'I came to the Prophet and found him asleep in a white dress. I came a second time and found him sleeping. On the third time he was awake. When I sat at his side he said: "Whoever says there is no God but Allah and dies in this belief will enter paradise."

I replied: "Even if he is an adulterer and a thief?"

He said: "Even if he is an adulterer and a thief."

(The question was asked and answered three times.)

The fourth time, Muhammad added: "Even if Abu Dharr was to turn up his nose."'

This Hadith does not suggest that as long as one believes in God all sins are forgiven. Both the Qur'an and the Hadith condemn theft and adultery. All such sins are forgiven if one sincerely repents, but the sin of not believing in one God is not forgiven.

a What important point do you think the Prophet Muhammad was trying to make in his final reply?

b Why do you think he used humour to make a serious point?

2 Read the Hadith below, and explain in your own words what each one is saying:

a *'God does not look upon your bodies and appearances; He looks upon your hearts and deeds.'*

b *'No one has eaten better food than what he earns with the toil of his own hands.'*

c *'Every one of you is a shepherd, and will be questioned about the well-being of his flock.'*

Look back

Hadith (page 7)

Angels

Muslims believe that there are four groups of beings in the universe:

- Humans.
- Animals.
- **Jinns** – spirits which are either good or bad.
- Angels – messengers sent by God.

Angels occupy a very important place in Islam. They were created from light by Allah in the beginning and so are God's servants, just as all human beings are. Angels love and obey Allah in all they do. Human beings, however, have been created with a free will to choose between right and wrong. Angels have not.

Angels are Allah's messengers and are present all the time. They are in touch with the **soul** of everybody. The Angel Jibril brought Allah's messages to the prophets. He delivered Allah's perfect word to Muhammad.

Guardian angels

When Muslims pray and think about God, they believe that angels are very close to them. Angels help Muslims to worship Allah in the proper way. They join with them in their prayers and give Muslims a feeling of peace and well-being.

Muslims believe that everyone has two guardian angels. They keep a record of everything the person has done. At the end of each prayer, Muslims turn to the right and to the left. One interpretation of this action is that they are recognising that their guardian angels are with them.

The special angels

There are several special angels mentioned in the Muslim holy books. Four of them are:

- Jibril – God's messenger who gave His word to the prophets.
- Israfil – in charge of the final destruction of the universe.
- Azra'il – the angel of death who is present at every deathbed to receive the soul.
- Mika'il – the guardian of all true believers who looks after every Muslim place of worship.

THERE IS NO GOD BUT ALLAH

AND MUHAMMAD IS HIS MESSENGER

BIRMINGHAM CENTRAL MOSQUE

How does Allah communicate with all Muslims?

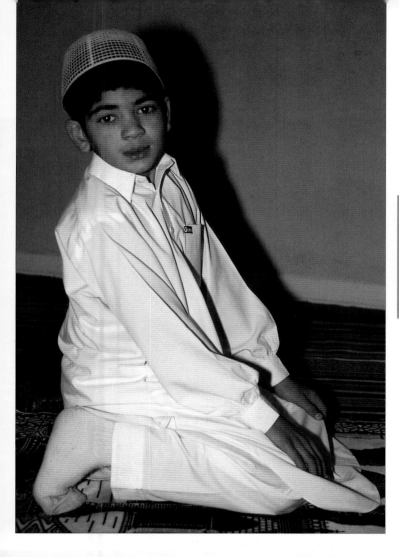

- What are jinns?
- What are guardian angels?
- How are humans and angels different?

For your dictionary

An **angel** is a spiritual being mentioned in the Qur'an and appointed by Allah to perform various tasks.
Jinns are spirits created by Allah and are made of fire. A **soul** is the spiritual part of a person, the part which worships Allah and survives after death.

Look back

Angel Jibril (page 11)

What might this Muslim be recognising at the end of his prayer?

1 Copy out this paragraph and fill in the missing spaces:

In the beginning, _____ were created by _____ and so are Allah's _____. The Angel _____ spoke to _____. Angels are in touch with the _____ of every believer. Each Muslim has two _____ _____.

2 In this crossword you have the answers but the clues are missing. Make up your own one-sentence clues to go with each answer.

Iblis

Iblis is the Islamic name for the devil. He is also known as Satan or Shaytan. After Allah had created the world, he commanded all His angels to bow down before Adam, the first man. They all did so, except one jinn – Iblis. Allah was displeased and banished him from paradise. Iblis said that he would tempt people away from God. God said that he would only succeed with people whose faith is weak.

Allah has millions of angels at His command – at least one for every human being. These angels are Allah's messengers. They carry out all His commands. They obey Him perfectly.

Iblis believed he was more important than Adam and refused to serve the human race as Allah commanded him to do.

Iblis argued with Allah, so Allah threw him out of heaven. This made Iblis very angry. He set out to destroy the human race by persuading people not to worship Allah. The way he does this is by:

- whispering wicked lies in the minds of men and women. Iblis tells them that they are equal to Allah. Too often they believe him.
- encouraging people to think that they can keep their sins secret from Allah. Yet Allah sees and knows everything. Nothing can be kept from Him.
- encouraging Muslims not to keep the laws laid down in the Qur'an.

Many Muslims respond to the tempting voice of Iblis instead of following God's guidance. This weakens their faith. The Prophet once said:

'My satan has surrendered to me and does only what I order him.'

This means that one should control evil desires.

Evil

Everyone knows that there is evil in the world. This evil causes great unhappiness. Much of this evil arises from the actions of human beings. God has created humans with a free will so that they can choose between right and wrong. Evil arises when a person chooses to do wrong. Evil is the result of people choosing the path of Iblis instead of the path of God.

Muslims believe that reading, and knowing, the Qur'an is able to save them from Iblis. Why do they think this?

Both the Qur'an and the Hadith tell people how they can be safe from evil. They must remember Allah all the time and follow the guidance of the Qur'an. The Qur'an shows people the paths of good and evil. Allah has also given people the power to think so that they can defeat Satan and chose the right path.

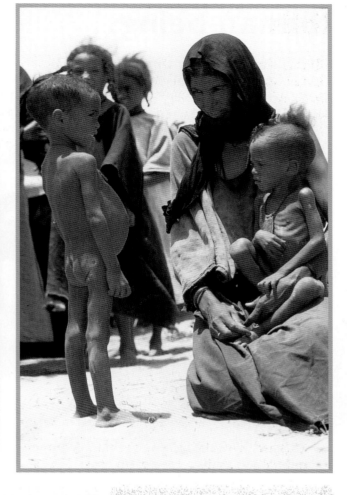

Who is responsible for suffering like this?

1 In your own words, write two sentences to answer each of these questions:

a Why did Allah throw Iblis out of paradise?

b What made Iblis angry with Allah?

c How does Iblis try to persuade human beings not to listen to Allah?

d How can Muslims protect themselves from the temptations of Iblis?

2 Read these two quotations from the Qur'an.

'"Lord," said Satan, "since You have thus seduced me, I will tempt mankind on earth: I will seduce them all, except those of them who are your faithful servants."' (Surah 15:39)

'"Begone!" said He [Allah]. "Hell is your reward, and the reward of those that follow you."' (Surah 17:64)

a What did Iblis decide to do after God had thrown him out of heaven?

b Which people are not tempted by Iblis?

c What is Iblis's final reward and who will join him there?

- Who is Iblis?
- Why is Iblis a great danger to the faith of Muslim believers?
- What happens if people choose the path of Iblis?

For your dictionary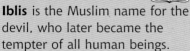

Iblis is the Muslim name for the devil, who later became the tempter of all human beings.

 Look back

Hadith (page 7)

Human beings

Muslims believe that when somebody comes to believe in Allah, their whole life changes. They now have the purpose and goal in life that they did not have before.

God's creations

All human beings have been created by Allah. Nothing happens to them by chance or accident. Everything and everyone is important. Those who appear to be the *least* important – the poor, the needy and the widows – are the *most* important to Allah. The Qur'an often asks people to believe in God and to do good. According to Islam, therefore, belief in God and doing good go together.

Human responsibility

Every Muslim carries enormous responsibilities both to Allah and to other people. To carry these out he or she must:

- feed those who are hungry and clothe those who are naked.
- look after those who are ill and injured – whether they are an enemy or a friend.
- protect the elderly.
- challenge evil wherever it is found – to do nothing in the face of evil is as bad as to commit an evil act.

Ummah

All human beings belong to one world. There are no special people. Everyone is equal. No one is more important than anyone else. The **ummah** is the worldwide community of Muslims who are united by their common beliefs and values. They are brought together by their shared spirit of unity and equality.

Within our own family we love our parents, children, brothers, sisters and grandparents. Belonging to Allah's family we have the same feeling towards everyone. They matter very much to us. When they are sad, we are sad. When they are in trouble, we try to help them out. When they mourn, we mourn with them. When they are excited and happy, we are the same.

What does a Muslim believe about the value of these people?

- Where is Allah in the world?
- What is ummah?
- What responsibilities does a Muslim have to Allah and to his fellow human beings?

For your dictionary

Ummah is the community of all Muslims, united by their common beliefs and values.

1 Look at these two photographs.

a What special responsibility does a Muslim have to the people here?

b Why do you think these people may need special protection?

c Try to list some of the ways in which the very young and very old are mistreated in today's world.

2 Here is a quotation from the Hadith. Read it carefully.

'To bring about a just reconciliation between two enemies is love, helping a person to mount his animal or load his baggage onto it is love, a good word is love, every step towards a mosque is love, to remove obstacles in the street is love, smiling upon the face of your brother is love.'

a This quotation from Muhammad's time gives seven examples of love in action. What are they?

b Write a paragraph of a similar length giving as many examples of what love might involve in the modern world. Is your paragraph very different from that of the Hadith?

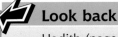 **Look back**

Hadith (page 7)
Mosque (page 17)

The prophets

There have been many prophets sent by Allah. Islam recognises twenty-four of them by name, including Ibrahim (Abaham), Yusuf (Joseph), Musa (Moses) and Isa (Jesus). The line of prophets ended with Muhammad. He was the last, and the greatest, of the prophets.

There are two Arabic words which describe a prophet:

- a **nabi** – a prophet sent by God to guide people to the right path.
- a **rasul** – a prophet sent by God to bring a revealed scripture to a community of people.

The line of prophets began with Adam. He was the first man on earth and the first of Allah's prophets. Adam's descendants soon spread. They were scattered over the earth. From them Allah chose many more prophets. He revealed His will to them. Through them Allah has guided His people. As the Qur'an says:

'God chooses for Himself whom He will, and guides to Himself whoever repents [makes amends].' (Surah 42:13)

Ibrahim

One of the earliest prophets was Ibrahim. When he was born in Ur of the Chaldees, many gods were worshipped in the city. He turned his back on all of them. Instead he saw the One God, Allah, behind all things. This God was invisible. For this reason, Ibrahim believed that it was foolish to make an idol or image to represent Him.

Musa

Musa was the only prophet to whom Allah spoke directly. All of the others were approached through the Angel Jibril. God gave Musa the Law to guide people according to his time.

Isa

Isa was a prophet sent by Allah. He was sent to the Jews who had strayed from the teachings of Musa. Muslims respect Isa as one of the great prophets sent by Allah to guide the people. They believe that he was not crucified, as the Bible claims, since one of his followers died in his place. Isa was taken directly up into heaven by Allah at the end of his life.

Muhammad

Muhammad, born some 600 years after Jesus, was the last of Allah's prophets. He was not God but was the last prophet of God.

Respecting the prophets

Out of respect for the prophets, no pictures of them are shown – whether in places of worship or in books. Instead, Muslims decorate places of worship with the most beautiful designs, such as calligraphy (elaborate handwriting), geometric designs and floral patterns.

- Who was the first prophet?
- What was unique about Musa as a prophet?
- How do Muslims show their enormous respect for the prophets?

1 Whenever a Muslim mentions a prophet, he always says: 'Peace be upon him.' Why do you think he does this?

2 Ibrahim came across King Nimrod in his travels. Nimrod regarded himself as being a god. Ibrahim told him:

'I acknowledge the Lord of the universe as my Lord and God of worship, and I disown completely the lordship and godship of everyone else.'

a Put the words of Ibrahim into your own words.

b Why do Muslims regard Ibrahim as a particularly important prophet?

3 These words about prophets come from the Qur'an:

'Say: "We believe in God and what is revealed to us; in that which was revealed to Ibrahim and Isma'il, to Ishaq [Isaac] and Ya'qub [Jacob] and the tribes; and in that which their Lord gave Musa and Isa and the prophets. We discriminate against none of them. To Him we have surrendered ourselves."' (Surah 3:84)

a Which prophets are mentioned by name in this extract?

b What does the Qur'an teach about the relationship between all the prophets?

c What do you think the Qur'an means when it says: 'To Him we have surrendered ourselves'?

Why do Muslims not draw or paint any of the prophets preferring, instead, to use patterns as a form of decoration?

For your dictionary

A **nabi** is the name for a prophet who is 'called forth' by Allah to carry His message.
A **rasul** is a popular title for Muhammad (the 'Rasul of God'), although it can be used of any prophet who brings a holy book from Allah.

Look back

Angel Jibril (page 11)

The ummah

Ummah is an important word in Islam. It was first used to describe Muhammad's companions in Madinah.
It is now used to describe the worldwide community of Muslims. Their common beliefs go beyond any differences that they might have.

This photograph of Muslims together shows you what is meant by 'ummah'. They may be male or female; their skins may be different colours; they may come from very different backgrounds and countries; they may speak many different languages. Something, though, unites them one with another. This is their common love of Allah, the One God, and Muhammad, Allah's prophet, together with their belief in the Qur'an and the Hadith.

Signs of ummah

At the heart of Islam, there are many activities which involve all Muslims. Take, for example, the following:

- The common practice of everyone facing the Ka'bah in Makkah when they pray. The Ka'bah is a symbol of that unity which links together Muslims everywhere.

- The Friday prayers when Muslims stand together as they pray. This emphasises their unity with each other.

How does this photograph show the bond that one Muslim has with another?

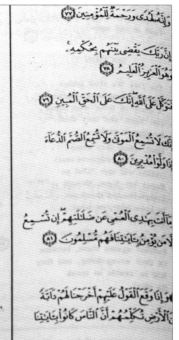

77. And it certainly is
A Guide and a Mercy
To those who believe.

78. Verily thy Lord will decide
Between them by His Decree:[3310]
And He is Exalted in Might,
All-Knowing.

79. So put thy trust in Allah:
For thou art on (the Path
Of) manifest Truth.

80. Truly thou canst not cause
The Dead to listen, nor
Canst thou cause the Deaf
To hear the call,
(Especially) when they
Turn back in retreat.[3311]

81. Nor canst thou be a guide
To the Blind, (to prevent them)
From straying: only those
Wilt thou get to listen
Who believe in Our Signs,
So they submit.

82. And when the Word is[3312]
Fulfilled against them (the unjust),
We shall bring forth from the earth

This page shows English and Arabic script from the Qur'an. How is learning Arabic an expression of ummah?

- Learning to recite and understand the holy book, the Qur'an, which all Muslims share together. Verses from the Qur'an, recited in Arabic, form an important part of the worship of all Muslims.

- The unity which all Muslims feel when they go on pilgrimage together on the **Hajj** to Makkah. On this journey everyone, rich or poor, is equal. All pilgrims show this by wearing the same simple clothes. On the Hajj, an animal is killed and the meat is shared with those who are too poor to buy an animal for themselves.

- The giving of money to the poor and to other good causes. This duty, called **zakah**, is a way of sharing one's wealth with others.

- How do Muslims express their unity with each other?
- How is the ummah between Muslims expressed on the Hajj?
- What is zakah?

Ummah is one of the most important things in a Muslim's life. It is the basis for many Hadith. Here are three examples:

- *'Each of you is a mirror of his brother; if you see something wrong in your brother, you must tell him to get rid of it.'*
- *'Believers are part of a building to one another – each part supporting the others.'*
- *'None of you can be a believer unless he loves for his brother what he loves for himself.'*

a What do you think it means to call a Muslim 'a mirror of his brother'?

b Describe two ways in which a Muslim supports other members of the faith.

c What do you love for yourself? Could you love the same things for other people?

For your dictionary
The **Hajj** is the pilgrimage to Makkah which every Muslim tries to make once in his or her lifetime.
Zakah is the duty of charity paid by Muslims to help support the poor and other good causes.

Look back
Hadith (page 7)
Ka'bah (page 13)
Madinah (page 13)
Ummah (page 39)

The Ka'bah

The Ka'bah ('cube') is the central shrine in Islam. It stands in the centre of the Great Mosque in Makkah. It is the only place in the world where believers pray in circles rather than in straight lines.

Who is said to have first built the Ka'bah?

Muslim tradition says that the Ka'bah was first built by Ibrahim and Isma'il, his son. It was restored by Muhammad, whose grandfather was, at one time, the guardian of the shrine.

By Muhammad's time, the Ka'bah contained more than 350 idols dedicated to many different gods. The Prophet Muhammad destroyed all of them when he returned to Makkah in triumph in 630 CE.

The Black Stone

The Ka'bah is built of granite (very hard, dark rock). It is twelve metres long, ten metres wide and fifteen metres high. In the south-east corner of the shrine, about one and a half metres above ground level, is set the Black Stone. This is said to have fallen from heaven. It was handed to Ibrahim by his son, Isma'il, when they were building the Ka'bah.

As the pilgrims walk around the Ka'bah on their pilgrimage they kiss or touch the Black Stone. This is a mark of respect for Allah.

The Ka'bah today

There is one door into the Ka'bah, in the north-east wall. During the Hajj, the inside is washed with rose water. The Ka'bah is empty except for gold and silver lamps which are hanging from the ceiling. The outside is usually covered by a thick, black cloth (called a robe), which is decorated in gold with verses from the Qur'an.

Why do you think that the inside of the Ka'bah is washed with rose water during the Hajj?

The Ka'bah as a symbol

Muslim tradition teaches that the Ka'bah is the centre of the earth. This means that it is the focus of Muslim unity. All Muslims turn towards the Ka'bah when they pray. There are many legends about the shrine: one is that it is the point where Allah's work of creating the world began.

- What is the Ka'bah?
- In what state did Muhammad find the Ka'bah – and what did he do about it?
- How would you describe the Ka'bah and the Black Stone?

1 Copy the drawing of the Ka'bah into your exercise book. Write two pieces of information about the history of the shrine underneath your drawing.

2 This photograph shows the Station of Ibrahim in Makkah. It contains a boulder on which Ibrahim is thought to have stood while he was building the Ka'bah. Why do you think it is important for Muslims to trace the history of the Ka'bah all the way back to Ibrahim?

3 The Qur'an has this to say:

'We made the House a resort and a sanctuary for mankind, saying: "Make the place where Ibrahim stood a house of worship." We enjoined [commanded] Ibrahim and Isma'il to cleanse Our House for those who walk round it, who meditate in it, and who kneel and prostrate themselves.' (Surah 2:124)

a What is the 'House' being referred to here?

b What does the word 'sanctuary' mean?

c Who was Isma'il?

d Who are those who 'walk round' the House?

e What is another word for 'meditate'?

f When do Muslims 'kneel and prostrate themselves'?

Look back

Black Stone (page 13)
Hajj (page 43)
Ka'bah (page 13)
Mosque (page 17)

The jihad

To Muhammad, Islam was a religion of peace and goodwill. While they lived in Makkah, his companions refused to fight against the enemies of the faith. However, in Madinah the Prophet began to teach that peace and goodwill have to go alongside courage, obedience and duty. **Jihad** means striving against evil and injustice for the sake of Allah.

Holy war

Islam is concerned to fight evil in the name of Allah. On occasions, this has involved actually going to war. The Qur'an teaches that this might be necessary. At the same time, it lays down the conditions of a 'holy war'. A 'holy war' could only be declared if those fighting:

- were trying to restore peace so that Allah could be freely worshipped.

- were defending the cause of Allah – fighting to gain more land or to conquer others was not allowed.

- were under the control of a spiritual and not a military leader.

Even then, other conditions were also imposed. Women, children, the elderly and the sick had to be protected. Every attempt must be made to protect civilians from harm. As little damage as possible was to be done to homes and crops.

In the past, Muslims have been accused of spreading their message through wars and fighting. The same charge has been levelled against all religions at some time. To do so would be completely against the teachings of Islam.

The Crusades were a series of wars in the eleventh and twelfth centuries involving Muslims and Christians. Find out a little about this time in history. Who claimed to be fighting a 'holy war'?

Injustice

Jihad is not simply a *physical* war; it is also a *moral* one. It aims to defeat those people who abuse or hurt others. It is a struggle to bring freedom and peace to those who are in need. It looks for every opportunity to spread peace. It accepts the teaching of the Qur'an that:

'Good deeds and evil deeds are not equal. Requite [repay] evil with good, and he who is your enemy will become your dearest friend.' (Surah 41:34)

Islam also teaches that there is a greater jihad. It is fought internally against the satan in one's mind. Controlling one's evil thoughts and desires is the greater jihad.

- What do Muslims mean when they speak of the jihad?
- Which groups of people need to be protected if a holy war breaks out?
- What does it mean to speak of jihad being a moral, as well as a physical, war?

What protection should be given to the innocent in a holy war?

Here are two comments about the jihad. Read them carefully:

'To me, the jihad is two things. It is a personal struggle in my own life against the sin to which I am prone. In the past it was also a physical struggle carried out by Muslims to establish our freedom to worship Allah.'

'The Qur'an teaches Muslims that they have a duty to encourage good and discourage evil. The Prophet said that the lesser jihad is to fight one's enemies but the greater jihad is to confront one's own evil desires.'

a What do you think are the sins to which everyone is prone in their private lives?
b Why do you think it was so important for Muslims to struggle in the past to achieve freedom of worship?
c Why do you think that Muhammad suggested that it was more important to fight one's own evil desires than to fight one's enemies?

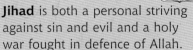

For your dictionary

Jihad is both a personal striving against sin and evil and a holy war fought in defence of Allah.

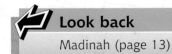

Look back

Madinah (page 13)

Akhirah

Muslims believe that life has two parts:

- The life that is lived on earth – and ends in the death of the body. This life is a kind of 'testing ground'.
- The life that is lived after death – and that has no end. This is called **eternal life** or **akhirah.** For akhirah, the body is brought back to life by Allah. Not all Muslims believe this: some believe akhirah is the life of the soul in the hereafter.

There is a strong link between the two parts of life. How we live in this life greatly affects what happens to us after we die. Our first life lasts for only a few short years. Akhirah is far more important and lasts forever.

'The value of this world in comparison to the hereafter is like a droplet in the ocean.' (Hadith)

On earth

Muslims believe that during each persons's life on earth, he or she decides their own fate. Through the many prophets, and particularly through the teaching of the Prophet Muhammad, Allah has shown everyone the way to heaven. If we follow their example and teaching, we will reach paradise. All that we need to do in this life is to reach out for Allah's forgiveness. This is given to all those who ask.

Each of us, though, has been given free will and by our actions in this life we earn our place in the next. Every person is responsible for his or her own destiny. We cannot do anything to help anyone else and no one can help us. A record is kept of everyone's behaviour. That book will be examined by the angels and by Allah at the end of time.

As Muslims believe that they must account for their actions to Allah, so this greatly affects the way that they live now. Knowing this helps them to think of others and be generous to those in need.

Why is the moment of death the last opportunity that Muslims have to affect where they will spend eternity?

A time for judgement

There is a time limit for everyone. It is in the present life that we have to face Allah. When life is over it is too late to do anything to alter God's judgement of us. Those who do not believe in Allah in this life will beg for a second chance. They will ask if they can go back to warn those they love – but there is no second chance.

The souls of those who die before the Day of Judgement are taken by Azra'il, the angel of death, to a waiting place. This is called **barzakh**.

- What is akhirah?
- How can people reach heaven?
- How does the belief in life after death affect the way that a Muslim lives now?

1 These statements are either true or false. If true, copy them into your book. If false, write out the correct version.

a A belief in life after death does not play an important part in Islam.

b The Arabic word for eternal life is akhirah.

c The lives that a person lives on earth and in eternity are totally separate from each other.

d The prophets, and especially the Prophet Muhammad, have shown everyone the way to paradise.

e People are not free to reach out for Allah's forgiveness in this life.

f Everyone is given a second chance after they die.

g Everyone's soul is taken by the Angel Jibril, the angel of death, to barzakh when they die.

Add two other statements of your own about the Muslim belief in life after death.

2 Copy and complete this crossword using the information given on these pages.

1 The spiritual part of a person, which leaves the body when we die.

2 It is God's _____ that decides what happens to us after death.

3 The life that is lived in heaven or hell is called _____ life.

4 The waiting place where every soul is taken after death.

5 The angel of death is called _____ .

6 The place of torment where all those without faith in Allah will go.

7 The future home of all true believers.

8 All those who ask for God's _____ will reach heaven.

9 Muslims believe that _____ has two parts.

For your dictionary

Akhirah is the Muslim belief that there is an unending life after death for every human being.
Barzakh is the place of waiting to which every soul is taken if they die before the Day of Judgement. The word means 'barrier'.
Eternal life is the unending life which is spent in either paradise or hell.

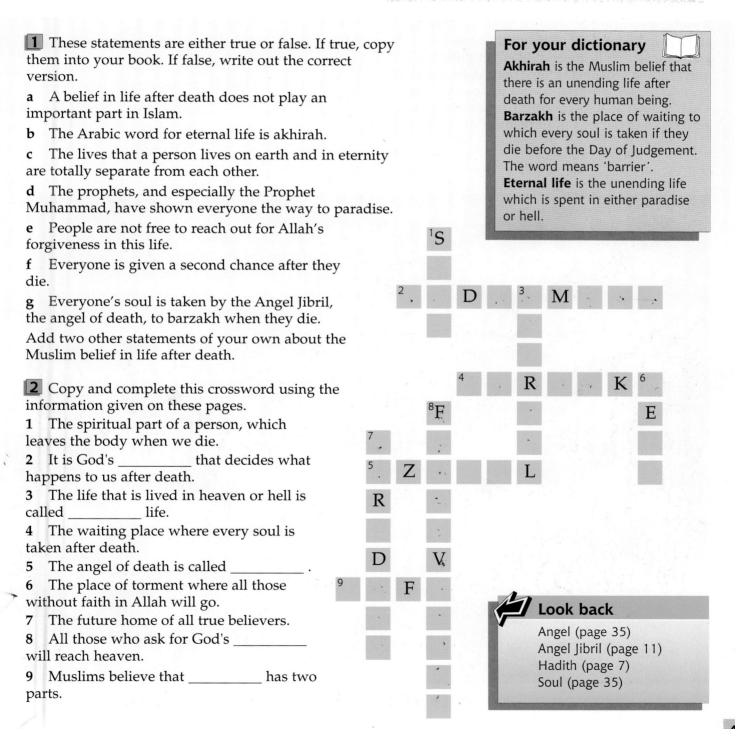

Look back

Angel (page 35)
Angel Jibril (page 11)
Hadith (page 7)
Soul (page 35)

The Day of Judgement

Both the Qur'an and the Hadith are quite clear. The Last Day, or the Day of Judgement, is coming. The time of the day is known only to Allah. On that day, the world as we know it will end and Allah will rule over everything.

Throughout history, Muslims have interpreted what the Qur'an tells us about the Day of Judgement, and heaven and hell, in different ways. Some Muslims believe that Allah will bring back to life the physical bodies of dead people. Others, such as sufis (mystics), believe that such references to the Day of Judgement are symbolic.

The end of the world

Most Muslims believe that what lies in store after death is completely unlike what we see, hear or feel in this world. The Prophet has said:

'Allah has prepared for His good people what no eye has seen, nor ear heard, nor has it entered into the heart of anyone.'

Muhammad then recited a verse from the Qur'an:

'No human being can imagine what blissful delights, as yet hidden, await them [in the life to come] as a reward for all they did.' (Surah 32:17)

Why do you think that many religions believe in hell?

The Last Day

On the Last Day two angels will question the souls about the lives they have led. Each soul will be rewarded or punished according to its deeds.

Hell

All those who do not believe in God and do evil will go to hell. Here they will suffer everlasting fear and shame. Hell is a place of scorching fire under the earth's crust. Those in hell are chained up with hot winds, boiling water and black smoke around them. They stay in hell forever.

'On the Day of Judgement, you will see all who invented lies against God [with] their faces darkened [by grief and shame]. Is not hell the [proper] abode for all who are given to false pride?' (Surah 39:60)

Heaven

Those who believe in Allah will go to heaven. The Qur'an tells us that it is like a garden with green plants, the sound of running water and birds singing. Both men and women will be taken up with the beauty of the nearness of God. It will be a place of great happiness.

'For those who do good, there is the ultimate reward and more than that. No darkness and no shame will come near their faces. It is they who are destined for paradise; they will abide therein.' (Surah 10:26)

No one can really know what heaven is like because no one knows what it is like to spend eternity in the presence of Allah.

---

1 Read the following statements and copy into your exercise book those which a Muslim would accept:

a Life on earth will end with the Day of Judgement.

b The souls of the departed will be judged according to the way they have lived in this world.

c The Day of Judgement will be accompanied by many terrifying natural events.

d Some people will escape the Day of Judgement altogether.

e All people will be questioned by two angels.

f All those who do not believe in God and evil-doers will go to hell.

g Hell is a place of unending torment.

h Paradise is another name for heaven.

i All who believe in God and who have done good will go to heaven.

2 Here are two quotations. Read them carefully and sum up in your own words what they say about the Day of Judgement:

'Would that you knew what the Day of Judgement is! Oh, would that you knew what the Day of Judgement is! It is the day when every soul shall stand alone and God will reign supreme.' (Surah 82:19)

'At evening do not expect to live till morning, at morning, do not expect to live till evening. Take from your health for your illness, and from your life for your death.' (Hadith)

- What will happen at the end of the world?
- What is the Last Day of which the Qur'an speaks?
- What are heaven and hell?

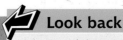

Look back

Angel (page 35)
Hadith (page 7)
Soul (page 35)
Sufis (page 9)

Meeting places (1)

Salah (prayers) may be performed in any clean place. Although Muslims can pray on their own, they prefer to pray with other believers. The Prophet Muhammad said that prayer in a congregation is many times more excellent than prayer said by a single person.

The Friday prayer is always said in a congregation and is performed at around midday. All adult male Muslims are expected to attend and, in Muslim countries, businesses close for the midday prayers. The Qur'an says:

'Believers, when you are summoned to Friday prayers, hasten [hurry] to the remembrance of God and cease your trading. That is best for you, if you but knew.' (Surah 62:9)

The mosque

By tradition, Muslims prefer to say their salah in a **masjid** (mosque) but this building is more than just a place of prayer. From the time of the Prophet, mosques have also been the centre of social life in the Muslim community.

When the Prophet came to live in Madinah, the Muslims there built a simple house of mud brick for him and his family. In its courtyard, there was a shelter which was used as a place of prayer. A wall or an object indicated the direction of Makkah, because Muslims face Makkah when performing salah.

The Prophet's masjid was also used for social purposes. He ran the affairs of the Muslim community from the building. The poor came to its courtyard for food and shelter. Visitors also used it as a place of rest when visiting the Prophet and people went there to recite and learn the Qur'an.

By tradition, therefore, the masjid has been used as a place for community gatherings, education and other social activities. The functions of mosques today follow the same pattern:

- Worship – prayer is the most important activity in a mosque.

- A meeting place – Muslims may meet in a mosque to celebrate the birth of a baby, a marriage or a funeral.

- Education – children and adults come to the mosque to learn Arabic and to study the Qur'an. In many mosques the children also learn other subjects in addition to the Qur'an.

This is a very simple mosque in Mauritania. What are mosques used for today?

Why is it true to say that a masjid is more than a place for prayer?

- Why do Muslims prefer to carry out salah with other Muslims?
- Which is the most important time of the week for salah?
- Which pattern are Muslims following when they build a masjid?

For your dictionary

The **masjid** is the Muslim place for prayer – the mosque.
Salah is the term used for formal prayers which are performed by Muslims five times a day.

1 Read this quote by the Prophet Muhammad:

'Wherever the hour of prayer overtakes you, you shall perform it. That place is a mosque.' (Hadith)

a What is a mosque?

b To what uses is a mosque put?

c What do you think Muhammad meant when he said this Hadith?

2 Muslims are told in the Qur'an that as God knows everything in the heavens and earth, three men cannot talk together in secret because Allah is the fourth. What do you think is the meaning behind this saying?

 **Look back**

Madinah (page 13)
Mosque (page 17)

Meeting places (2)

Mosques have remained essentially the same for centuries. As Islam has spread to different parts of the world, however, so other features have been added. These have enriched the lives of Muslims in the country.

Mosques are built in different styles. Many mosques are beautiful buildings, but they all contain the same basic features:

- A prayer hall in which prayers are performed. This hall faces Makkah, as Muslims face in this direction when they pray. The direction of Makkah is called the **qiblah**.

- A higher platform or pulpit, the minbar, from which the sermon at Friday prayers is delivered.

- Washing facilities for worshippers to perform **wudu**. These facilities may be in a courtyard or inside the building.

The mosque may also have other features. Before prayer begins, believers are called together. This call to prayer is called the **adhan** and it is delivered by the **mu'adhin** five times a day. In many mosques the adhan is delivered from a high tower called the **minaret**, although the mosque built by the Prophet did not have minarets. Many mosques also have a dome. Minarets and domes were later additions, and they are not essential for a mosque.

Why might a mosque have minarets?

Inside the mosque

When Muslims enter a mosque to pray, they remove their shoes. This is a sign of respect for the house of Allah. There are no seats inside, so, on entering the prayer hall, Muslims sit on the floor or on their **prayer mats**. The design of these mats always includes an arch which is placed to face the direction of Makkah.

There are no pictures or statues inside a mosque. Muslims

Why are no pictures or statues allowed in a mosque?

believe these may distract those worshipping. Worshippers should think only of Allah. The walls and pillars, however, are often highly decorated with beautiful patterns of verses from the Qur'an.

Muslims believe that the greatest value is found in saying prayers together in a mosque. However, if a Muslim cannot attend the mosque, prayers can be said in any clean place. The Prophet said that the whole world is a mosque.

- What is the qiblah?
- How do prayers begin in a mosque?
- What happens if a Muslim cannot attend a mosque for prayers?

1 These two photographs show features that are found in many mosques. What are they called?

2 What part do the adhan and the mu'adhin play in Muslim prayer?

3 Imagine that you go into the prayer hall of a mosque whilst prayers are being conducted. Make a list of five things that you are likely to notice.

For your dictionary

The **adhan** is the call to prayer given by the mu'adhin five times a day.

A **minaret** is a high tower from which the call to prayer is sometimes given.

The **mu'adhin** is the person who calls the faithful to prayer five times a day.

A **prayer mat** is laid out by a Muslim so that he or she can pray in a clean place.

The **qiblah** indicates the direction of Makkah so that Muslims can face the holy city when they pray.

Wudu is the ritual washing that always takes place before prayer.

Look back

Mosque (page 17)

Meeting places (3)

Muslims go to masjids to say their salah along with other believers. In addition to salah, Muslims also have other forms of prayer and services. These are also said in mosques but, by tradition, Muslim communities meet in their own places of gathering for these additional services.

Such services include **du'a**, **dhikr** and the singing of poems. They are often held in places of gathering that are different from mosques. As people who gather for these services also go to the mosque for salah, so all these places complement each other. In fact, they have existed side by side for centuries.

Amongst the earliest of such places is the **ribat**. According to Muslim tradition, the first ribat was built in the seventh century, during the time of the second caliph, Umar. To begin with, a ribat was a fort on the frontier. Its function was to defend Muslim communities against enemy attacks.

People who defended a ribat were volunteers and their leader was a sheikh, a holy and learned person. The volunteers were deeply religious people who spent much of their time studying and praying. Gradually, the ribat changed from being a fort to a place of special prayer and studying. The people who gathered there were often sufis.

Sufi and Shi'ah communities

Sufi communities in different countries have had their own places of gathering for many centuries. These places are known by different names, the most common of which is 'khanaqah'. In Turkey, a similar place is called a 'tekke' and in North Africa it is known as a 'zawiya'. Over the years the words have all come to mean the same thing.

Services and lessons in khanaqahs take place under the leadership of the sufi sheik. Khanaqahs often serve as a shelter for the poor as well as a place to which people can go for advice and help with their problems.

According to a famous sufi sheikh in India, khanaqahs were inspired by the Qur'an. One verse of the Qur'an says:

'[Lit is such a light] in houses which God has permitted to be raised in honour; for the celebration, in them, of His name: In them He is glorified in the mornings and in the evenings.' (Surah 24:36)

A famous sufi scholar, Ghazzali, said that anyone could enter a ribat to share its food once or twice, because it is a sufi custom to be hospitable. This shows that, unlike mosques, such places have been mainly private but they are meant for private and personal forms of worship.

Shi'ah communities also have their own places of gathering in which they hold devotional services. Such buildings also serve as community centres for educational and social activities.

This ribat is in Tunisia. When was the first ribat built?

- What is a ribat?
- How has the ribat changed over time?
- What is a khanaqah?

For your dictionary

Dhikr refers to the remembrance of Allah in one's heart or by reciting His names or sections from the Qur'an.

Du'a are the personal prayers said by Muslims. The word itself means 'asking'.

A **ribat** was once a fort on a frontier and is now a meeting place of sufis.

A khanaqah in Morocco. By what other names are khanaqahs known?

Answer each of these questions in your own words using the information on these pages.

a   Why do Muslims go to mosques?
b   When was the first ribat built?
c   What was the function of the early ribats?
d   What do we know about the volunteers who manned the early ribats?
e   By which different names are the alternative sufi places of gathering known?
f   What are Shi'ah places of gathering used for?
g   What are people invited into a ribat for and why?

Look back

Masjid (page 53)
Mosque (page 17)
Salah (page 53)
Sufis (page 9)

The imam

The word 'imam' means leader or guide. An imam is someone who leads Muslims in their prayers in a mosque. For Shi'ah Muslims, the imam is the direct descendant of the Prophet Muhammad and the spiritual leader of the community.

The imam as leader of prayers

The imam does not have any special training for his work. He is not 'ordained' like a Christian priest or a Jewish rabbi. As all Muslims are equal, no one can represent them in Allah's presence. They must stand before God on their own.

Imams are chosen from the congregation that they serve. They must have a solid background in the faith and be leading a life as a Muslim which is an example to others.

The imam as community leader

Shi'ahs believe that just before Muhammad died, he appointed Ali, his cousin and son-in-law, to be his successor. Ali became the first imam of the believers. Shi'ahs believe that since the time of Ali, there has always been a heriditary imam from the family of the Prophet to guide them. He interprets the message of Allah for each age. The Prophet said:

'I am the city of knowledge and Ali is its gate.'

The work of the imam

Apart from leading prayers in the mosque, especially on Fridays, the imam also delivers a sermon to the people. The sermon is given either from a pulpit (the minbar) or from a special seat. This sermon is called the khutbah.

The imam also carries out other tasks:

- He teaches people of all ages in the mosque about the faith. His work with children is very important. Not only does he talk to them about Islam, but he also teaches them Arabic – the language in which the holy books are written.
- He performs some religious ceremonies, such as name-giving and marriage, although other members of the Muslim community can also do this. He often gives people religious advice.
- He works among the Muslim community. For example, he might visit Muslims in prison or in hospital.

Why is the imam standing in front of these worshippers?

In small Muslim communities the imam is likely to have another job to support himself and his family. However, in the larger communities, being an imam is a full-time occupation. The very largest mosques may have more than one imam to look after the congregation.

- What does the word 'imam' mean?
- What is the main task of the imam?
- What kind of person must the imam be and from where is he chosen?

When does the imam deliver a sermon from his seat in the mosque?

Monday 4th
9.00–11.00: Deal with mosque business with secretary.
11.30: Meet local police inspector – community relations.
2.30: Visit Mrs Khan in hospital.
6.00–10.00: Youth club in mosque.

Tuesday 5th
Day off – visit family in Leicester.

Wednesday 6th
9.00–12.00: Prepare sermon for Friday prayers.
2.00: Visit Shan Muhammad in prison.
3.30: Speak to other Muslims in prison.
5.00–7.00: Counselling class in mosque.

Thursday 7th
10.00–12.00: Visit library and bookshop on mosque premises.
2.00: Funeral.
4.00: Wedding in mosque.

Friday 8th
1.30–2.00: Friday prayers.

Saturday 9th
11.00: Wedding.
1.00–3.00: Teach in weekend school.
5.30: Meeting of Islamic parents–teachers' association.

Sunday 10th
10.00–3.00: Weekend school for children.
4.00–6.00: Arabic class for adults.

This page is taken from the diary of an imam in Britain. It shows a typical week in his life. He is responsible for a medium-sized mosque and works full-time as an imam.

a How would you describe an average week in the life of an imam?

b Make a list of all the different activities that this imam carries out in a typical week.

 Look back

Ali (page 7)
Imam (page 7)
Khutbah (page 31)
Mosque (page 17)

Shahadah

Muslims have five important beliefs. These are called the **Five Pillars of Islam**. Each belief is like the pillar of a building – each pillar is important in itself, but remove any one of them and the building will fall down. These pillars are the duties which every Muslim is expected to carry out. They are:

- The **Shahadah** – the belief that there is only one God and that Muhammad is His messenger.
- Salah – to pray five times each day.
- Zakah – giving money to the poor.
- **Sawm** – fasting during the month of Ramadan.
- Hajj – the pilgrimage to Makkah, the holy city.

The Shahadah is the Muslim declaration of faith in Allah. It is the pillar on which all the others are based. Without it the other pillars would mean nothing. Muslims believe that, 'There is no god but Allah and Muhammad is His messenger.'

When a person can say the Shahadah and mean it totally in their hearts they are a true Muslim. A Muslim will say the Shahadah thousands of times during his or her lifetime. In particular, they will:

- repeat it many times each day between getting up in the morning and going to bed at night.
- whisper it into the ear of their new-born baby.
- teach it to their children as soon as they are old enough to learn it.
- hope that it will be the last words to cross their lips before they die.

Whose example is this mu'adhin following as he calls the faithful to prayer in a mosque?

Muhammad arrived in the city of Madinah in 622 CE. One of his earliest companions was Bilal, a converted Abyssinian slave. Muhammad told him to call the faithful to prayer five times a day. Bilal used the words of the Shahadah to do so. These words still form part of the call to prayer that the mu'adhin delivers five times daily. The full Sunni call to prayer is:

'God is great! (four times)

I bear witness that there is no god but God. (twice)

I bear witness that Muhammad is the Prophet of God. (twice)

Come to prayer! (twice)

Come to success! (twice)

God is great! (twice)

There is no god but God.' (once)

(The Shi'ahs add 'Come to perform the best of deeds' twice after the fifth line.)

What is the Shahadah?

1 The Shahadah plays a very important part in the life of every Muslim. Why do you think:

a they repeat it many times a day, especially first thing in the morning and last thing at night?

b they whisper it into the ear of every new-born baby?

c they hope it will be the last words they say before they die?

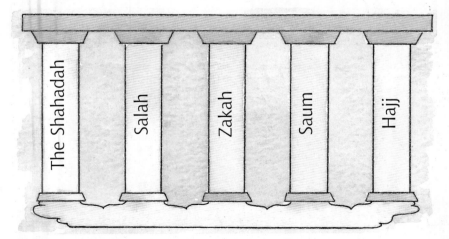

2 a Why do you think Muslims think of their five duties as five pillars?

b What would happen if one of the pillars was weakened?

- What are the Five Pillars of Islam?
- What is the call to prayer and who gives it?
- What makes a person a true Muslim?

For your dictionary

The **Five Pillars of Islam** are the five basic duties of every Muslim.

Sawm is the practice of fasting, which happens in the month of Ramadam.

The **Shahadah**, the first of the Five Pillars of Islam, is the statement of belief in Allah and Muhammad, His Prophet.

Look back

Bilal (page 19)
Fast (page 19)
Hajj (page 43)
Madinah (page 13)
Mosque (page 17)
Mu'adhin (page 55)
Ramadan (page 9)
Salah (page 53)
Zakah (page 43)

Preparing for prayer

Muslims do not find it easy to live as witnesses to Allah. There are so many other things that crowd their lives. If they wish, therefore, to be truly committed to Allah, some real discipline is needed. That is why they are encouraged to perform salah five times every day. During that time, their thoughts are turned away from everyday things to Allah.

A Muslim can say his prayers in public or private. In practice, he will use a combination of the two. He can pray at any time and Allah will hear him. Salah is a unique kind of prayer that is carried out five times a day. This is the special time set aside for Allah.

Wudu

Salah begins with washing (called wudu). In the courtyard of a mosque there are special washing facilities. There is a difference between everyday washing and performing wudu. Wudu always follows the same pattern, which begins with the worshipper announcing his intention to offer the prayer to Allah. This announcement is called **niyyah**.

a The hands are washed three times.

b The mouth is rinsed three times.

c The nostrils are washed out three times. The face is then washed three times.

d The arms are washed as far as the elbows three times.

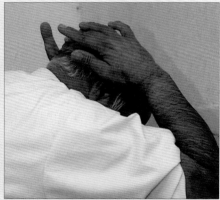

e The top of the head, the ears and the back of the head are washed.

f The feet are washed as far as the ankle three times.

g The shoes or sandals are left outside before entering the mosque to pray.

Why do you think that the body of a person must be clean before they can pray to Allah?

Salah

Salah does not have to take place in a mosque. It can be carried out in any public place as long as:

- the person is clean. If no running water is available for wudu then clean sand will do.
- the place is clean. Muslims use a prayer mat to make sure of this. All prayer mats have a directional arch on them, which is pointed towards Makkah.

- What is wudu?
- What is the first stage of wudu?
- How and why are prayer mats used?

1 The washing of the body before salah is very elaborate. It can take several minutes. Why do you think the Qur'an insists on running water being used for this?

2 Read this quotation about prayer:

'Aby Huraira reports that he heard the Prophet say: "If one of you has a river at his door in which he washes himself five times a day, what do you think? Would it leave any dirt on him?" The companions said: "It would not leave any dirt on him." The Prophet said: "This is an example of the five prayers with which Allah blots out the evils of a man."' (Hadith)

On more than one occasion, the Prophet Muhammad said that praying was like washing in a stream. What do you think he meant?

For your dictionary

Niyyah is the intention to do something.

 Look back

Hadith (page 7)
Mosque (page 17)
Prayer mat (page 55)
Salah (page 53)
Wudu (page 55)

Rak'ah (1)

To perform salah, Muslims follow a sequence of movements. This involves standing, bowing or kneeling face down on the floor (called 'prostration'). Each cycle of movements is called a **rak'ah.**

Rak'ahs must be done at each of the times set aside for salah during the day. The exact number of rak'ahs performed varies from two to four. depending on the time of the day.

Before the prayer sequence begins, Muslims must make their devotion to Allah clear by saying the Shahadah. Without the person's heart being in the right place, everything else is worthless.

b Standing upright, Muslims raise their hands to the level of their shoulders. All distractions from the world around and from within are shut out. They say: 'Allah is great'.

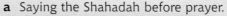

a Saying the Shahadah before prayer.

On these pages you can see the first four movements that go to make up one rak'ah. You will find out about the remaining actions in a rak'ah in the next chapter.

- What is a rak'ah?
- What does a Muslim need to do before he begins a rak'ah?
- What is the Fatiha?

For your dictionary

The **Fatiha** is the title of the first surah in the Qur'an, Its meaning contains the whole essence of the holy book.
A **rak'ah** is a sequence of movements that is followed during salah.

c The hands are placed on the chest with the right one on top of the left. The **Fatiha** is recited. This includes the words: 'You alone we worship, and to You alone we turn for help'. Any other passage from the Qur'an may then be recited.

d Bending from the hips, keeping the back straight and spreading the fingers on the knees, Muslims are showing that they respect and love God. These words are said three times: 'Glory be to my Great Lord and praise be to Him'.

1 Here are two quotations:

'Woe to those who pray but are heedless [thoughtless] in their prayer; who make a show of piety [devotion] and forbid almsgiving [charity].' (Surah 107:6–7)

'When a person is drowsy during prayers, let him sleep until he knows what he recites.' (Hadith)

a What dangers does the Qur'an warn all worshippers to avoid when they are praying?

b What should a person do if they are tired when he or she comes to prayer?

2 Look closely at the four photographs on these two pages. Draw up a table like the one below and fill in the information.

Photo	Action	Words spoken
a		
b		
c		
d		

Look back

Salah (page 53)
Shahadah (page 61)
Surah (page 29)

Rak'ah (2)

There are five more movements left in the rak'ah. Both the words and the movements are based on an example set by the Prophet Muhammad. Together they symbolise total obedience to Allah.

The first movements of the rak'ah are given on pages 64 and 65. For those actions, the worshipper has remained on his or her feet.

f Muslims go down on their knees, bend forward, and with their forehead, nose and both hands to the ground, say: 'Glory be to my Lord, the Most High, God is greater than all else'. This position is called prostration and shows their love of God above all else.

1 Look closely at the five photographs on these two pages. Draw up a table like the one below and fill in the information.

Photo	Action	Words spoken
e		
f		
g		
h		
i		

e Muslims stand upright and say: 'God listens to those who thank Him. O Lord, thanks be to you'. They are showing that they are aware of God's presence with them.

h At this point, they prostrate themselves again by repeating the actions and words in **f**. Finally, the rak'ah is either repeated or finished.

g They then kneel up again with the palms of their hands resting on their knees. They rest for a moment before saying these words three times: 'O my Master, forgive me'.

i The final movement is for each worshipper to look to the right and to the left. This is to show respect for the other members of the congregation and for the guardian angels. These words are said: 'Peace be with you and the mercy of Allah'.

2 Read this quotation by Muhammad:

'The prayer said in Madinah is worth thousands of others, except that in Makkah, which is worth a hundred thousand.

But worth more than all this is the prayer said in the house where no one sees but God, and which has no other object than to draw close to God.' (Hadith)

a Why are Makkah and Madinah mentioned as the two places in which prayers are so valuable?

b What was Muhammad referring to when he spoke of the 'prayer said in the house'?

c What is the one object of prayer which is worth more than any other?

- What do the movements and words in a rak'ah symbolise?
- What is prostration?
- What is different about the final movement in a rak'ah?

 Look back

Angel (page 35)
Hadith (page 7)
Madinah (page 13)
Rak'ah (page 64)

Du'a

Like many things in life, prayer needs to be worked at. As the Qur'an says:

'Attend regularly to your prayers, including the middle prayer, and stand up with all devotion before God.' (Surah 2:239)

Muslims do not have to go to the mosque to pray. Prayers can equally well be said at home. Many Muslims pray privately to Allah whenever they want to. Personal prayers of this kind are called du'a. These prayers are said in addition to salah.

There are many occasions in life when a Muslim wants to say some extra prayers. These occasions may include:

- during Ramadan. During this month of fasting, a Muslim's thoughts turn naturally towards God, and so saying extra prayers is helpful.
- when a long and difficult journey is about to be undertaken.

- after a blessing has been received from Allah – a recovery from illness, the birth of a baby, the end of troubled times, the opening of a new business, etc.
- when someone is in need of help, forgiveness or guidance.

Sometimes a Muslim might use a set prayer as a du'a. At other times he may pray in the way that he feels he needs to. There is no set time for these prayers. The prayers can be of any length and can take place anywhere. They can be in the language of the worshipper.

Tasbih

Sometimes a Muslim holds a string of beads between his fingers to help him pray. Each bead represents one of the 99 names of Allah. The string is called a tasbih. After performing the rak'ahs, a Muslim may decide to praise Allah using his beads. After each bead he will say: 'Glory be to Allah', 'Thanks be to Allah' or 'Allah is great'.

What do you think these travellers might have prayed to Allah about before setting off on their journey?

This is what the words 'In the Name of God' look like in Arabic. This is called the **Bismillah**. Why do you think this is a particularly important part of every Muslim prayer?

- What is the main difference between salah and du'a?
- What kind of things might lead a Muslim to seek God's guidance in a du'a?
- What is the Bismillah?

Muslims may pray to Allah about everything. At the same time, they always remind themselves that God knows everything about everyone:

'You should worship Allah as if you are seeing Him; for He sees you, even if you do not see Him.' (Hadith)

Copy these two paragraphs into your book, filling in the missing words as you go:

During _____ a Muslim may want to say some extra prayers. He can pray in any place, at any time. It may happen when he is worried about something or when he needs guidance from _____.

Sometimes a Muslim may stay behind after the _____ to praise God using a string of beads called _____. This will help him to remember the _____ names of _____. Prayers of this kind are called _____.

This man is using a tasbih. What does each bead represent?

For your dictionary

The English translation of the **Bismillah** is 'In the Name of God'.

Look back

Du'a (page 57)   Fast (page 9)
Hadith (page 7)   Mosque (page 13)
Rak'ah (page 64)   Ramadan (page 9)
Salah (page 53)   Tasbih (page 27)

Zakah

Giving money to the poor (zakah) is one of the Five Pillars of Islam. Time and time again it is stressed in the Qur'an as a duty for every Muslim. In some Muslim countries the government collect it as a tax and then give it away to the poor. In others, it is collected by the local mosque.

In Islam, compassion and generosity are very important. Muhammad was an orphan himself. The Qur'an says that as Allah helped Muhammad as an orphan, Muslims should help orphans and those who need support.

Paying zakah

Paying zakah is a spiritual act. The word itself means 'purity'. Muslims believe that they do not own anything since everything has been lent to them by Allah. As Allah has given the wealth to them, so every Muslim must give generously to those in need.

At the end of each year, every Muslim must give $2\frac{1}{2}$ per cent of his or her savings as zakah. This, though, is only the minimum – there is no limit. But a Muslim must provide for his own family first. Anything left over after doing this is additional wealth and the amount of zakah to pay is based on this.

Zakah is a blessing

Zakah is not intended to take away the money and wealth of people. Like other duties, paying zakah is a blessing to all Muslims.

Paying zakah is an obligation, but the Qur'an and the Hadith also recommend the voluntary giving of time, skills, knowledge and money to help those in need. The Qur'an and the Hadith also teach that the poor should try to be self-reliant.

Paying zakah is a test of honesty – a Muslim cannot live happily with himself if he does not pay zakah. He knows that he will have to answer to Allah on the Day of Judgement. The Qur'an tells him that a complete record of his deeds is being kept in heaven. That record will show if he has been generous and honest.

These people are paying zakah. Why do Muslims believe that it is their duty to pay part of their savings as zakah?

- What is zakah?
- Why was Muhammad particularly concerned about the poor and needy?
- How should those who receive zakah look on the gift that is given to them?

1 Read these quotations from the Hadith:

'*He is not a believer who eats his fill while his neighbour remains hungry by his side.*'

'*One who manages the affairs of the widow and the needy is like one who exerts himself hard in the way of God.*'

Explain in your own words what each of these Hadith is saying.

2 This extract is from the Qur'an:

'*Attend to your prayers and render the alms levy [pay zakah]. Whatever good you do shall be rewarded by God. God is watching all your actions.*' (Surah 2:110)

a State one reason why praying and giving to the poor should be linked together.

b What do you think the Qur'an means when it says, 'Whatever good you do shall be rewarded by God'?

What responsibilities does a Muslim have towards the poor?

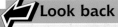**Look back**

Five Pillars of Islam (page 61)
Hadith (page 7)
Mosque (page 13)
Zakah (page 43)

Sawm

All good things in life, including food, come from God. Allah has given them to all believers to enjoy. However, one month of the year – Ramadan – is set aside for fasting. During this month, Muslims do not eat or drink anything during daylight hours. This is called sawm and it is one of the Five Pillars of Islam.

The festival of Ramadan celebrates the time when the Prophet Muhammad received his first revelation from the Angel Jibril. This happened on a night towards the end of Ramadan – known to Muslims as the Night of Power.

On this night the angels came down and blessed all those who remembered Allah. Muhammad's wife noticed that on this day he prayed harder than on any other day.

What happens during Ramadan?

Every Muslim must fast during Ramadan since this is their duty to Allah. The only people who are not expected to fast are:

- the very old.
- those under the age of 12.
- those who are ill.
- those who are expecting a baby or breast-feeding one.
- those who are travelling.

Apart from the very young and the very old, the others are expected to make up the fast as soon as possible.

If food is a gift from Allah, why do you think it is a good idea to go without it for a time?

Why fast?

There are several reasons why Muslims fast during Ramadan. Some of them are because:

- it builds up self-control and prevents greed.
- it reminds all Muslims of what it is like to be poor and hungry. Hunger is the same for everyone, so it is important to share the experience.
- it brings together Muslims from every background and reminds them that they are all equal in the sight of Allah.
- it gives Muslims more time to pray, to read the Qur'an and to help the poor.

Why do you think Ramadan is likened by Muslims to the experience of travelling through the desert?

- What is sawm?
- Which event in the life of Muhammad is the inspiration for Ramadan?
- How long does Ramadan last?

1 This quotation from the Qur'an explains the importance of fasting for Muslims:

'Believers, fasting is decreed [ordered] for you as it was decreed for those before you...Fast a certain number of days...In the month of Ramadan the Qur'an was revealed, a book of guidance for mankind...But he who is ill or on a journey shall fast a similar number of days later...God desires your well-being, not your discomfort...He desires you to render [give] thanks to Him for giving you His guidance.' (Surah 2:183–6)

a What is fasting?

b Which month is set aside for Muslims to fast?

c Why is this month so important for all Muslims?

d Which groups of people within the Muslim community are not expected to fast during Ramadan?

e This extract suggests one spiritual blessing to be had from fasting. What is it?

2 The Qur'an indicates when a fast should begin and when it should end:

'Eat and drink until you can tell a white thread from a black one in the light of the coming dawn. Then resume the fast till nightfall...' (Surah 2:187)

This offers a simple test to show when the fast should begin and when it should end.

a Explain in your own words what this test is.

b Why do you think such a guide was necessary when the Qur'an was written?

Look back

Angel (page 35)
Angel Jibril (page 11)
Fast (page 9)
Five Pillars of Islam (page 61)
Ramadan (page 9)
Sawm (page 61)

Id-ul-Fitr

The month of Ramadan is over. There now follows a festival which marks the end of Ramadan. This festival is called Id-ul-Fitr. This brings the whole Muslim community together for a time of prayer and celebration. Id-ul-Fitr is celebrated in different ways in different countries. Here is how one community in Britain celebrates this festival.

Before the festival begins, Muslims pay zakah. This is the time when they give money to the poor so that they can buy some food for the festival celebrations. No one should go hungry during Id-ul-Fitr.

Few people go to bed on the last night of Ramadan. They meet other Muslims on the street to watch the new moon rising. Early the next morning, Muslim families gather (usually in a mosque) to thank Allah for the blessings they have received during Ramadan. The imam tells them in his sermon that they must look after the poor members of the community. Allah has given them this duty. He also tells them that Allah promises His followers two things things for having completed the fast:

- The pleasure they feel once the fast has ended.
- A reward from Allah on the Day of Judgement.

Why do Muslims celebrate the festival of Id-ul-Fitr?

Celebrating Id-ul-Fitr

After the service everyone goes home – often to a family party. Houses are decorated with Id-ul-Fitr cards and these often carry the words 'Id Mubarak' ('Have a happy and blessed festival'). Presents are sometimes given and special cakes and sweets are enjoyed by the children. Many Muslims visit relatives for the celebration. A traditional pudding of dates and milk may be eaten.

Both Ramadan and Id-ul-Fitr are important reminders to all Muslims. By fasting during Ramadan, Muslims are reminded that their worldly needs are less important than their love for Allah. Fasting unites all Muslims, rich or poor, in their effort to tame the worldly desires and to purify their souls. The Id gives them the pleasure of enjoying the good things in life and reminds them of the spiritual rewards of fasting.

One last thing remains to be done – a visit to the cemetery. Everyone wants to remember those who can no longer enjoy the celebrations. A complete Muslim family includes both the living and the dead.

- What is the link between Ramadan and the festival of Id-ul-Fitr?
- What signals the start of Id-ul-Fitr?
- What two rewards are promised to those who complete their fast in Ramadan?

1 These cards are typical of those sent during Id-ul-Fitr. Design and make your own Id-ul-Fitr card that would be suitable to send to a relative or a friend.

2 The following words can be found horizontally, vertically or diagonally in the wordsquare below. Find and circle each one and then write two or three paragraphs to sum up the festival of Id-ul-Fitr.

Zakah	Month	Moon
Community	Id Mubarak	Ramadan
Bless	Allah	Duty
Id-ul-Fitr	Presents	Mosque
Poor		
Fast		
Food		
Festival		
Eat		
Reward		
Pay		
Imam		
Celebrate		

```
R  Z  C  O  M  M  U  N  I  T  Y
P  A  Y  F  B  L  E  S  S  I  C
R  K  M  O  N  T  H  X  D  D  E
E  A  O  A  I  Y  E  N  D  M  L
S  H  O  L  D  M  O  S  Q  U  E
E  P  N  L  U  A  A  M  D  B  B
N  O  Q  A  L  E  N  M  U  A  R
T  O  B  H  F  A  S  T  T  R  A
S  R  S  A  I  T  T  R  Y  A  T
A  F  E  S  T  I  V  A  L  K  E
F  O  O  D  R  E  W  A  R  D  Z
```

For your dictionary

Id-ul-Fitr is the festival which comes at the end of the month of Ramadan, marked by many celebrations in the Muslim community.

Look back

Fast (page 9)
Imam (page 7)
Mosque (page 13)
Ramadan (page 9)
Zakah (page 43)

The Hajj (1)

The word 'Hajj' means 'to undertake a journey with a definite purpose'. The pilgrimage to Makkah, which almost every Muslim undertakes, is called the 'Hajj'. Any man who completes the journey is known as a 'hajji' and any woman is a 'hajjah'.

Every Muslim who is healthy and can afford it tries to go on the Hajj once in their lifetime. Only those who are old, sick, disabled or poor are not expected to go on the religious journey.

Before they go, each pilgrim must provide for his or her family at home. If they fail to do this, the Hajj will not be of any spiritual benefit to them.

The Hajj is a deeply spiritual experience for every Muslim. They visit Makkah and Madinah, the holy cities most closely associated with Islam. There they experience the warmth of travelling and praying with two million other Muslims. Every pilgrim wears the same clothes as a symbol that they are all equal in the sight of Allah.

Why do you think it is important that all pilgrims are dressed in similar clothes?

Ihram

The Hajj takes place each year during the twelfth month of the Muslim calendar. Pilgrims travel to the city of Makkah from all over the globe. On the outskirts of the city they enter a holy state – **ihram**. Ihram involves taking off their normal clothing and putting on special clothes:

- Men and boys wear two white, unsewn cotton sheets. One of these is tied around the waist and the other is draped over the left shoulder.

- Women and girls put on a long, plain dress and a head-covering. Veils which cover the face are not allowed on the Hajj.

Ihram also means that from this time onwards all pilgrims are forbidden to:

- use any perfume or perfumed soap.
- wear any jewellery (but women may wear wedding rings).
- have any sexual relations.
- cut their hair or nails.
- kill any living thing, including plants.

All of this puts each pilgrim in the right spiritual frame of mind to undertake the Hajj.

This photograph shows pilgrims gathered around the Ka'bah in Makkah. What do you think pilgrims might gain from being with so many other fellow-believers?

- What is the Hajj?
- What is ihram?
- What are the rules of ihram?

1 Is there someone in your area who been on a Hajj? If so, it would be interesting to invite them in to answer your questions about the pilgrimage. You might like to find out, for example:

a why they went on the Hajj in the first place.

b how they travelled to Makkah.

c what the holy city of Makkah is really like.

d which places, other than Makkah, they visited and what they did there.

e what it was like being part of such a large pilgrimage.

f what they gained spiritually from making the Hajj.

2 Many pilgrims keep their Hajj clothes so that they can be buried in them. Give two reasons why a Muslim might want to do this.

For your dictionary

Ihram is the first stage of Hajj, in which pilgrims enter a holy state and put on special clothes to show equality and purity.

 **Look back**

Hajj (page 43)
Ka'bah (page 13)
Madinah (page 13)

The Hajj (2)

When they reach the outskirts of the city of Makkah, many Muslims find themselves speechless. Others weep and are overcome with emotion. Some experience overwhelming feelings of joy. For every pilgrim, a lifetime's ambition has been realised.

The Hajj

Only Muslims are able to enter the city of Makkah. The first thing that every pilgrim does when he reaches the city is to head towards the Ka'bah. He will walk or run around the shrine seven times in an anti-clockwise direction, saying a prayer each time. Each lap starts from the Black Stone. He kisses the Black Stone or raises his arms to it each time he goes round the Ka'bah. His thoughts are now just of Allah.

The Qur'an says that the Ka'bah was first built by Ibrahim and his son, Isma'il. Muhammad cleared all of the idols out of the Ka'bah. From then onwards it was used only to worship Allah. Some Muslims believe that it lies directly beneath the throne of Allah in heaven.

During the Hajj, the Ka'bah is covered by a large, black cloth. At the end of each Hajj this cloth is cut up into small pieces and sold to pilgrims as a memento of their pilgrimage.

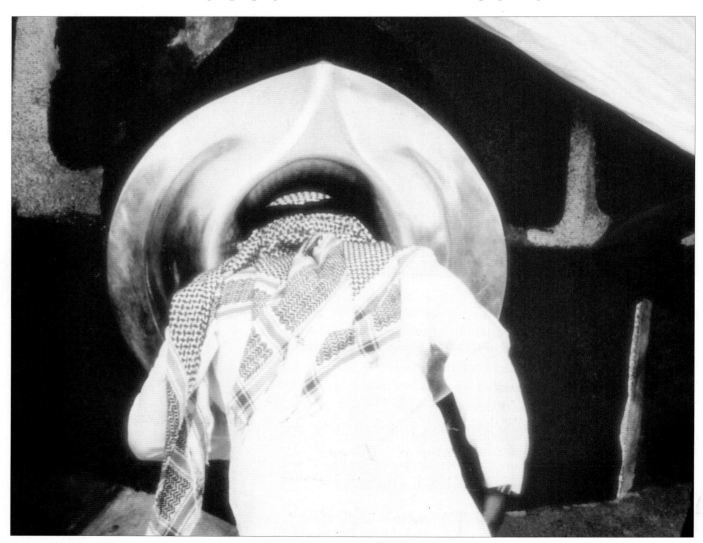

This pilgrim is kissing the Black Stone. What is the Black Stone and why is it important?

The next part of the Hajj is the sa'y. This means walking seven times between two small hills, Marwa and Safa. This is to remind pilgrims of Hajar. Hajar was Ibrahim's wife, who ran between the two hills in search of water for her son.

Pilgrims then travel to the plain of Arafat and the Mount of Mercy, where Muhammad preached his last sermon. The pilgrims stand here and pray from noon until sunset. This is the most important part of the Hajj.

Before ending the Hajj, pilgrims go on to Mina, where they spend three days. On each day, they throw seven stones at each of three pillars. The pillars symbolise the devil. This reminds Muslims of Ibrahim's refusal to listen to the devil.

After the Hajj

The Hajj is now over and the pilgrims must return to Makkah to go around the Ka'bah once more. Ihram is then over.

Some pilgrims travel on to the tomb of Muhammad in Madinah. That is a long journey of 482 km from Makkah. Others return home to share the blessings of the Hajj with those who did not go.

- What do pilgrims do at Marwa and Safa?
- What happens at Mina?
- What is the most important event during the Hajj?

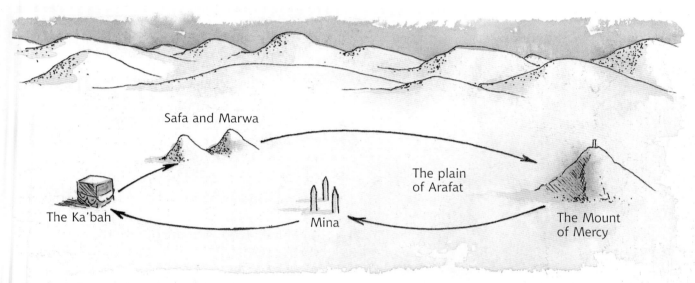

Safa and Marwa

The plain of Arafat

The Ka'bah

Mina

The Mount of Mercy

1 a Copy this map into your exercise book.

b Explain what happens during the Hajj at each of the places shown on this map.

2 This is a brief impression by a hajji. Read his description through carefully.

'There were all kinds of people on the Hajj – men and women, black and white, young and old, rich and poor. That was the first thing I noticed. I also discovered that everyone had gone with the same purpose in mind – to renew their commitment to Allah. I did that, too. The great joy for me was to travel with so many other Muslim brothers and sisters. We had only one goal.'

a What was the first thing he noticed as he made his pilgrimage to Makkah?

b What discovery did he make about the purpose that everyone had in mind?

c Why do you think he felt 'great joy' on the Hajj?

Look back

Black Stone (page 13)
Hajj (page 43)
Ihram (page 77)
Ka'bah (page 13)
Madinah (page 13)
Mount of Mercy (page 25)

Id-ul-Adha

Id-ul-Adha is a festival which begins on the tenth day of the Hajj. At the heart of the festival is the idea of service and sacrifice. This is the spiritual meaning behind the sacrifice of an animal. When an animal is sacrificed, its deeper meaning is that one should always sacrifice one's own selfishness. Only when this happens can a person submit to Allah. This is how Ibrahim submitted himself to God.

Long before Muhammad was born, there was a prophet called Ibrahim. He was ready to sacrifice his own son, Isma'il, to show that he was willing to obey Allah completely. However, at the last moment, Allah provided a ram for sacrifice instead. Ibrahim had been tested by Allah and had proved his faith. Id-ul-Adha is all about each Muslim committing himself or herself totally to Allah.

The feast of sacrifice

At the centre of the festival of Id-ul-Adha is the sacrifice of an animal. Each family must select a perfect animal (a sheep, goat, cow or camel) to be sacrificed. In many cases, the father will slaughter the animal himself. In countries like Britain, however, this is not allowed. Animals have to be killed in an abattoir (slaughter house).

Strict conditions are laid down for the slaughter of the animals:

- The animal must not be frightened.
- The animal must be turned to face Makkah as the slaughterer calls on the name of Allah.
- Prayers from the Qur'an are read out.
- A very sharp knife is drawn across the jugular vein of the animal.
- All of the blood is drained from the animal. Muslims believe that it is unclean to eat the blood of an animal.

Meat which is killed in the correct way is called **halal**.

Once the sacrifice has been made, the meat is cut up. The family that has provided the animal keeps one-third of the carcase for its own needs. The remainder of the carcase is given to relatives and to the poor and needy. This is often the only time of the year that the poor have meat to eat.

- What does Id-ul-Adha remind Muslims about?
- What is the link between the Hajj and the festival of Id-ul-Adha?
- What is at the heart of the celebration of Id-ul-Adha?

Why do you think that only a perfect animal can be sacrificed to Allah?

1 In this extract, a Muslim is describing the importance of the festival of Id-ul-Adha:

'To go on the Hajj you have to make many sacrifices. These sacrifices are an important part of the meaning of the pilgrimage. The idea of making a sacrifice is also at the heart of the festival of Id-ul-Adha. Both those who go on the pilgrimage and those who stay at home want to be reminded of Ibrahim. He was prepared to sacrifice his own son if Allah demanded it. It reminds all Muslims that they must be prepared to sacrifice everything for Allah.'

a What sacrifices do you think people who go on the Hajj make?

b Do those who stay at home also make a sacrifice to help others? If so, what kind of sacrifice is it?

c How does the story of Ibrahim and Isma'il fit in with the idea of sacrifice?

d In the modern world, what extreme sacrifice might a Muslim be called on to make?

This shop is selling halal food. How are animals killed in order to produce halal meat?

2 In this crossword, you have the answers but not the clues. Make up your own clue to go with each answer.

For your dictionary

Halal is any action or thing which is allowed or lawful.

Look back

Hajj (page 43)

Between birth and death
Childhood

All babies born into a Muslim family are gifts from Allah. They are welcomed into the ummah – the worldwide family of Islam – soon after they are born. This family will look after them throughout their lives.

Birth

After the birth, the father of the child takes it into his arms. He whispers the adhan, the call to prayer, into its right ear:

'God is great! I bear witness that there is no god but God. I bear witness that Muhammad is the Prophet of God. Come to prayer! Come to success! [The Shi'ahs add 'Come to perform the best of deeds!'] God is great! There is no god but God.'

This means that the name of Allah is the first word that the new baby hears. After the adhan has been recited, a tiny piece of sugar or date is placed on the baby's tongue by an elderly relative. This expresses the hope that the baby will grow up to be kind and considerate.

What is this man whispering into the ear of his new-born baby?

The aqiqah ceremony

Seven days after the birth of the baby, some Muslim communities perform the **aqiqah** ceremony. Several important things may happen at this time:

- The child's head is shaved. This symbolises the removal of all misfortune. Gold and silver equivalent to the weight of the hair is given to the poor and needy.

- A sheep or a goat may be sacrificed. A third of the animal is eaten by the family and the rest is given away to the poor.

- The child is given its name. In Islam, a person's name is very important. Many children are named after Allah, Muhammad or one of the other prophets.

- If the baby is a boy, **circumcision** will probably take place at the same time. Boys can, however, be circumcised at any time up until their tenth birthday.

The Bismillah ceremony

In some Muslim countries, the Bismillah ceremony is held when a child is exactly four years, four months and four days old. It marks the first time that the Angel Jibril appeared to Muhammad. It is the start of the child's religious education, when he or she learns the first sentence of the Qur'an off by heart:

'In the name of God, the Compassionate, the Merciful.'

Muslims take the religious education of their children very seriously. It begins, as we have seen, with the Bismillah ceremony. It continues at the madrasah – the school in the mosque.

A relative places a small piece of sugar on the baby's tongue. Why do you think he is doing this? What does he, and everyone in the family, hope for the baby?

- What do Muslims do when a new baby is born into the family?
- What happens at the aqiqah ceremony?
- What is the Bismillah ceremony?

1 a Why do you think that a person's name is so important in Islam? Could there be a link between a person's name and the kind of person they turn out to be?

b Why do many Muslim names come from Allah, Muhammad or one of the other prophets? What might the parents be hoping for when they choose such a name?

c Why do you think an animal might be sacrificed at the aqiqah ceremony?

2 At the Bismillah ceremony, some verses from the Qur'an are read to the child, who then repeats them:

'Recite in the name of your Lord who created – created man from clots of blood. Recite! Your Lord is the Most Bountiful One, who by the pen taught man what he did not know.' (Surah 96:1)

a What happens at the Bismillah ceremony?

b Why do you think these words are appropriate to read at this time?

For your dictionary

Aqiqah is the ceremony at which a baby is named.
Circumcision is the removal of the foreskin of a boy's penis.

Look back

Adhan (page 55)
Angel Jibril (page 11)
Bismillah (page 69)
Madrasah (page 31)
Mosque (page 13)
Ummah (page 39)

Arranged marriages

Muslims strive to lead a balanced life by observing their worldly and religious responsibilities. The family is an important means of reaching this balance. Marriage, therefore, plays an important role in Muslim communities and Muslims are encouraged to raise families and to look after them.

There are many ways in which marriages take place in Muslim communities. They vary from one place to another, depending on the culture and country in question.

Finding a partner

Arranged marriages are a matter of custom amongst Muslims and non-Muslims. Muslim tradition does not demand that a Muslim marriage is arranged by parents and relatives. Some Muslim communities and families, however, prefer to have arranged marriages. They ensure that the consent of the boy and girl is sought before the arrangements are made.

Some Muslims marry by finding their partners out of their own free choice. They may meet them at work or they may be introduced through their friends and acquaintances.

Preparing for marriage

There are various ways in which Muslim communities make preparations for a marriage. If it is an arranged marriage, the parents of the man and woman will meet to discuss the preparations. If the couple have chosen one another, they will inform their families of their decision. The families will then help them as they prepare for marriage.

The families of the couple reach an agreement on the **mahr**. This is a sum of money or goods that the bridegroom gives to the bride to show his commitment to the marriage. The size of the mahr depends on the status of the bride and groom, and the way it is paid varies in different Muslim families and communities.

Soon, the engagement and the date of the wedding are announced. The families and relatives prepare for the wedding ceremony and the celebrations that will follow.

The bride's father and the bridegroom shake hands during the ceremony. Why do you think Islam stresses that marriage is more than the coming together of two people – it is the uniting of two families?

Are all Muslim marriages arranged?

When asked about arranged marriages, a young Muslim replied:

'In Muslim communities, marriage is much more than the uniting of two people. It is the bringing together of two families and so many more people are involved. Also, as young people, we need to draw on the wisdom of those older than us before making such an important decision. That is why divorce is very rare in Muslim countries.'

a What do you think are the main arguments for and against arranged marriages? Copy this table into your exercise book and list your arguments from the most important downwards. (You might like to spend some time discussing this with others in your class first.)

Arguments for	Arguments against

b Do you think that the wisdom of older people could be very useful in deciding whom a person should marry?

- What is an arranged marriage?
- What is a mahr?
- How do Muslims find their marriage partners?

For your dictionary

A **mahr** is a sum of money or goods which the bridegroom agrees to pay the bride before a marriage takes place.

Marriage

Getting married in the Muslim community is a simple and straightforward matter. The ceremony can take place anywhere – although, in Britain, it is usually performed by the imam in a mosque. The wedding is not a religious ceremony. It is carried out in accordance with the laws of the country in which it is performed.

The Qur'an expects a couple to grow in love throughout their married life. This is Allah's clear intention for every man and woman. As the Qur'an says:

'He [Allah] gave you spouses [husbands and wives] from among yourselves, that you might live in peace with them, and planted love and kindness in your hearts.' (Surah 30:20)

More than one wife?

According to some interpretations, the Qur'an allows a man to have up to four wives at the same time. He must treat all his wives fairly and equally. He must not favour one over the others. In practice, though, few Muslim men have more than one wife. It usually only happens if:

● the first wife is unable to have children, *or*
● the first wife is so ill that she needs help to run the home.

● Why might a Muslim man feel the need to take more than one wife?
● What is a marriage contract and why is it so important?
● What does the Qur'an hope for every newly married couple?

This woman is about to get married. What might some of her hopes be for her married life ahead?

A person belonging to a particular faith usually marries another of the same faith. Why do you think this is?

The marriage contract

When a Muslim couple marry, a wedding contract is drawn up. This is very important. A woman can insist in it that her husband does not marry anyone else. The contract also lays down a sum of money which must come from the husband's family. This remains the wife's if the couple later divorce. This contract is called the **nikah**.

The wedding ceremony

There is no official Muslim wedding ceremony. The couple can marry in a mosque or at home.

They follow local customs. The important thing is that the marriage contract is signed by the bridegroom and the bride or the bride's male guardian (usually her father or a close relative). This signing must take place in front of two male Muslim witnesses.

In many communities, an imam does not have to be present at the wedding. If he is, however, he will say a few words to the couple as they set out on their married life together. The couple then lead a procession from the bride's old home to the couple's new home.

As part of the wedding ceremony, the couple are asked three times if they agree to marry each other and they exchange rings. The imam, or someone else, blesses them with the words:

'In the Name of God, the Compassionate, the Merciful.'

Why do you think:

a the couple are asked three times if they consent to the marriage?

b the couple exchange rings?

c the couple are blessed in the name of Allah?

For your dictionary

The **nikah** is the wedding contract signed by the bridegroom before a Muslim wedding.

 Look back

Imam (page 7)
Mosque (page 13)

The place of women

In Islam, all men and women are equal in Allah's sight. The Qur'an addresses Muslims as both the 'believing men' and the 'believing women'. This is because God's message as revealed in the Qur'an applies to both men and women.

Women in Islam

Before the birth of Islam, in most societies in the world, women were less important than men. When Muhammad began preaching Islam in Arabia, he sought to improve the position of women. He forbade Muslims to kill newly born female babies, which was an Arab custom at the time. He guided Muslims to look after the widows who had no protection or support. Muhammad also allowed women to own property and to run their own businesses.

In the years that followed, there were many women who played a leading role in the Muslim community. Khadijah was the Prophet's wife and the owner of a caravan train. The Prophet's daughter, Fatima, was actively involved in helping the poor and needy in Madinah. Muslims also respect Aisha, one of the wives of the Prophet who played an active role in the Muslim community after his death.

In the centuries that followed, women continued to play a prominent role. They were rulers, jurists, poets and mystics. Some of them were wealthy patrons who gave money to build and maintain mosques, schools and hospitals. Ibn Rushd, a famous Spanish Muslim in the twelfth century, insisted that men and women were equal in ability. It was only local custom which often denied women the chance to study and, instead, forced them into domestic life.

Women today

Today, Muslim women are actively involved in all kinds of work. Some women, for example, have become prime ministers in their home countries. Others hold senior government positions as ministers and ambassadors. Muslim women are also involved in the teaching and medical fields, with many others running their own businesses. Muslim women writers have written and published books which are read the world over.

Find out how the prayer-life of a Muslim woman differs from that of a man.

What kinds of posts might Muslim women fill in today's societies?

1 Muhammad told his companions:

'Modesty and faith are joined closely together; if either of them is lost, the other goes also.' (Hadith)

What do you think he meant?

2 This verse comes from the Qur'an:

'The believers, men and women, are protectors of one another. They enjoin what is just, and forbid what is evil. They observe regular prayers, pay alms [money] regularly, and obey God and His messenger. God will have mercy on them. God is Mighty and Wise.' (Surah 9:71)

a Why do you think that both men and women are addressed in this verse from the Qur'an?
b What are the responsibilities of Muslim men and women?

- How did Muhammad improve the position of women in his time?
- What has been the role played by women in Muslim history?
- In what different fields are Muslim women engaged today?

 Look back

Hadith (page 7)
Khadijah (page 13)
Madinah (page 13)
Mosque (page 13)

Food and drink

With the exception of a few things, Muslims are free to eat and drink whatever they like. God says in the Qur'an:

'O you who believe! Eat of the good things which We have provided you, and give thanks to Allah if it is He whom you worship.' (Surah 2:172)

Most foods are lawful for Muslims to eat. Eating the pure and wholesome foods that Allah has provided is a spiritual duty. A good and wholesome diet is necessary for everyone. It is also part of an individual's commitment to Allah.

Forbidden food

There are, however, some forbidden foods and liquids. The Qur'an forbids a Muslim to consume:

- any meat whose method of slaughter is unknown – all meat eaten by Muslims has to be slaughtered according to strict rules.

- pigs (or anything made from a pig).
- an animal that has been killed in the name of anyone other than Allah.
- any flesh-eating animal.
- any meat containing blood.

All of the above are **haram.** All food that Muslims are allowed to eat is halal.

In practice, then, a Muslim is not allowed to eat pork (or anything like lard or sausages that includes pork products). He is allowed to eat all fish and poultry products, together with the meat of sheep and game. Chicken and lamb are amongst the most popular foods.

However, the Qur'an does allow for an exception to be made. If the choice is between eating the forbidden foods and starving, the person should eat. The laws are laid down to help the health and well-being of the Muslim community – not to act as a burden to it.

What does it mean to call this a 'halal' foodshop?

Halal	**Haram**

What is the main reason for the food laws laid down for the Muslim community?

Alcohol

According to the Qur'an, the date palm and the vine provide fresh fruits, date honey and vinegar. The intoxicants which cause so much damage to individuals and to society come from rotted, fermented fruit.

Alcohol, or any other drug which impairs one's mind, is discouraged in Islam. Alcoholism is one of the major problems that many communities and societies face today.

- What does 'haram' mean?
- Which animals are allowed for food and which are forbidden?
- Why are Muslims discouraged from drinking alcohol?

1 Imagine a Muslim family of father, mother and three children aged 18, 15 and 7 living in Britain. What problems do you think each member of the family might have in keeping the Muslim food and drink laws, whilst living a normal life in Britain?

2 Read this extract from the Qur'an carefully:

'He has forbidden you carrion, blood, and the flesh of swine; also any flesh that is consecrated [blessed] other than in the name of God. But whoever is compelled through necessity, intending neither to sin nor to transgress [disobey], shall incur no guilt. God is forgiving and merciful.' (Surah 2:173)

a List the things that this extract states are forbidden to Muslims.

b What happens to those who *have* to eat the forbidden foods?

For your dictionary

Haram is any action or thing which is not allowed or unlawful.

Look back

Halal (page 81)

Old age

As people grow old they need special care and attention. In Muslim communities, this love is given by the family. There are many passages in the Qur'an and the Hadith which encourage Muslims to look after their parents when they grow old. The care of old people is never passed over to someone outside the family. That would be unthinkable.

Extended family

In some parts of the world, especially in rural areas, Muslims may have **extended families**. In an extended family, brothers, sisters, uncles and aunts live close together. In large cities, Muslims may live in smaller families consisting of parents, children and sometimes grandparents. But wherever they live, Muslims like to keep in touch with their relatives.

Grandparents

The head of a Muslim family is always the eldest person. Age is always respected, so grandparents are important. Children are taught to be respectful to their parents and to their grandparents. The Qur'an gives this advice to children about treating their parents with proper respect:

'Your Lord has enjoined [told] you to worship none but Him, and to show kindness to your parents. If either or both of them attain old age in your dwelling [house], show them no sign of impatience, nor rebuke [find fault with] them; but speak to them with kind words. Treat them with humility [respect] and tenderness and say: "Lord, be merciful to them. They nursed me when I was an infant."' (Surah 17:23–4)

Within the extended family it is accepted that the older members will be able to do less and less. They may become confused and bed-ridden. Their children, though, are taught to always treat them with tolerance and respect.

In what ways would you expect the oldest members of this family to help those who are younger?

Why are Muslims told to treat the older members of their family with such great respect?

1 Read this quotation:

'May his nose be rubbed in dust who found his parents approaching old age and did not enter paradise by serving them.' (Hadith)

a How does this Hadith suggest someone will enter paradise?

b Why do you think that looking after one's parents is placed so high on the list of priorities?

2 Answer the following questions in your own words:

a How are children in a Muslim family expected to show love and respect for their parents?

b Is there any suggestion that an age can be reached when a person no longer has such a responsibility?

c Do you think that living in an extended family makes it easy to look after family members when they grow old?

- What is an extended family?
- Who is the head of an extended family?
- Why do children have a big responsibility to their parents?

For your dictionary

An **extended family** is when a family of several generations live either under the same roof or very close to each other. Extended families may be large and include many relations.

 Look back

Hadith (page 7)

Death and burial

It is reported that, as Muhammad approached death, he said:

'Allah, help me through the hardship and agony of death.'

He also asked Allah for forgiveness.

As they approach death, Muslims try to follow Muhammad's example. As they believe strongly in life after death, they try to face death without fear. After death, they believe that their souls enter eternal life to be reunited with the souls of those they have loved. The Qur'an says:

'To God we belong, and to God we will return.' (Surah 2:156)

What is the Shahadah and why does it bring comfort to the person who is dying?

All Muslims hope that they will be able to recite the Shahadah before dying so that their sins can be forgiven. Relatives and friends gather around the bedside. They read passages from the Qur'an. They say prayers and ask Allah to be merciful to the dying person.

After death

After death, the body is washed in scented water. This can be done by the husband or wife or someone of the same sex. The body is then dressed in white robes – three for a man and five for a woman. If they have visited Makkah on the Hajj, their robes can be used.

After death, all people – rich or poor – are treated in exactly the same way. Everyone is equal in God's sight. The body is taken to the mosque or an open space for the funeral prayer. The prayer contains the words:

'O God, pardon this dead person; lo, Thou art the Most Forgiving, the Most Merciful.'

Muslims do not cremate their dead – everyone is buried. In Muslim countries, a coffin is usually not used as the body should be buried in contact with the earth. It is laid with the right side facing Makkah and the head turned in the same direction.

As a person is buried, handfuls of earth are dropped into the grave. What reason can you suggest for this?

Mourning

The Prophet Muhammad wept when his son died. Muslims are not afraid to show their feelings when someone has died. They mourn for the dead person for between seven days and three months. After burial, it is believed that the grave is visited by two angels who question the dead person to see whether they are fit to enter paradise.

This photograph shows a body being handed down into a grave. Why do Muslims prefer not to use coffins?

- What happens to comfort a person as death approaches in a Muslim family?
- How do Muslims prepare a dead body for burial?
- What do Muslims believe happens after death to see whether a person is fit to enter paradise?

Muslims believe that after a person has died, two angels visit the grave. They are there to examine a person's fitness to face Allah on the Day of Judgement. Mourners at the graveside may recite this verse:

'O male or female servant of God, remember the covenant [vow] made while leaving the world, that is the attestation [confirmation] that there is no God if not God Himself, and that Muhammad is the Messenger of God, and the belief that paradise is a verity, that hell is a verity, that the questioning in the grave is a verity, that the Day of Judgement shall come, there being no doubt about it – that God will bring back to life those who are in the graves, that thou hast accepted God as thy Lord, Islam as thy religion, Muhammad as thy prophet, the Qur'an as thy guide, the Ka'bah as thy direction to turn to for the service of worship and that all believers are thy brethren [brothers]. May God keep thee firm in this trial.'

a What do you think a 'verity' is? How many verities are mentioned here and what are they?

b There are several characteristics of the true Muslim who can look forward to the Day of Judgement with confidence. What are they?

Look back

Angel (page 35)
Eternal life (page 49)
Hajj (page 43)
Ka'bah (page 13)
Mosque (page 13)
Shahadah (page 61)
Soul (page 35)

Index

Page references in bold indicate that the word is defined on this page in the 'For your dictionary' box.